IBRIK

THE BALKAN TABLE

Now or never: this is our motto. And now, after months of collaboration, we have this book in our hands. Grégoire Seguin, you are the person I always dreamed of having in my corner! In such a short time, you were able to make this culture your own.

ECATERINA PARASCHIV

ECATERINA PARASCHIV

IBRIK

THE BALKAN TABLE

PHOTOGRAPHY BY ÉMILIE FRANZO

Smith Street Books

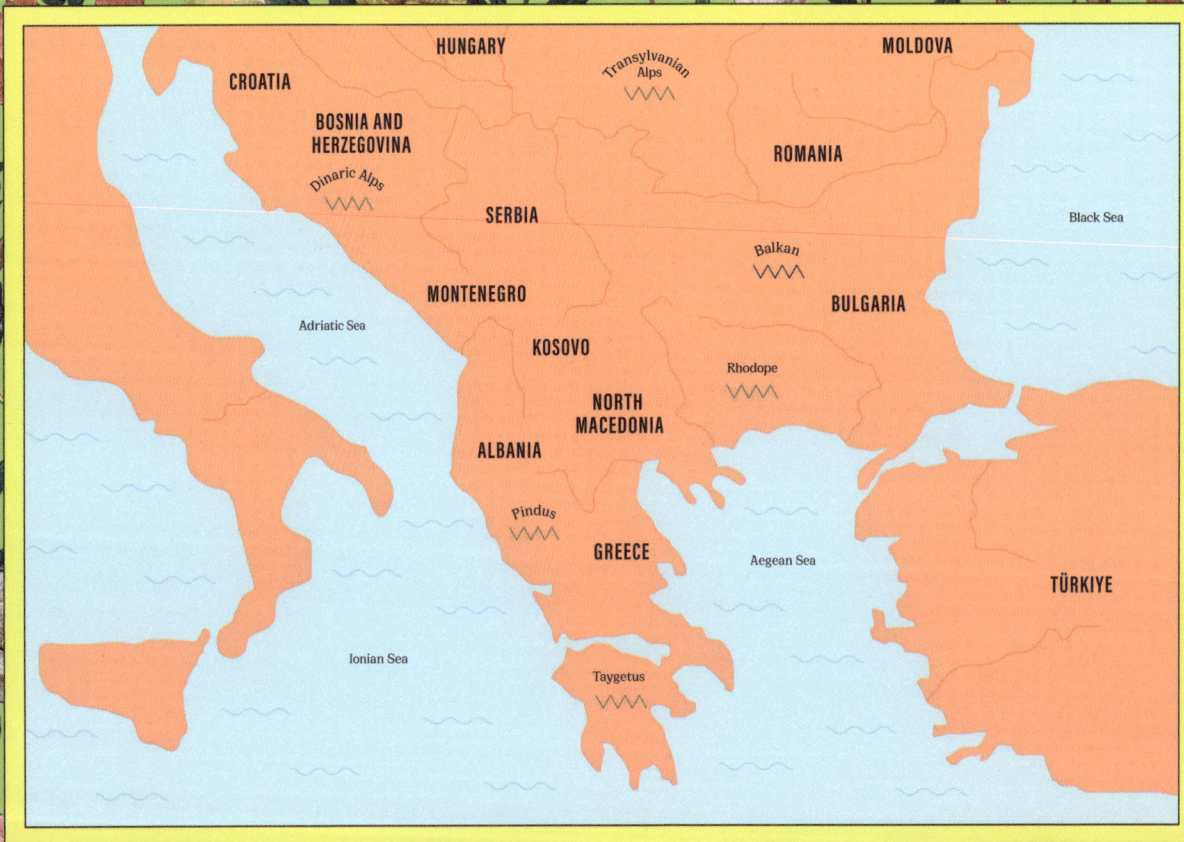

CROATIA

HUNGARY

Transylvanian Alps

MOLDOVA

BOSNIA AND HERZEGOVINA

Dinaric Alps

ROMANIA

SERBIA

Black Sea

Balkan

MONTENEGRO

BULGARIA

Adriatic Sea

KOSOVO

Rhodope

NORTH MACEDONIA

ALBANIA

Pindus

GREECE

Aegean Sea

TÜRKIYE

Ionian Sea

Taygetus

CONTENTS

MY BALKAN CUISINE

Around the lands of the Balkans, there exists a fog almost as thick and dense as the clouds that surround Mount Olympus – one that leaves no clear definition of the land or the people who live there, with their values, beliefs and culture. On a map, it's difficult to trace the region's contours or draw clear borders that define it with any certainty. Though I was born in these lands, even I still don't truly know all of their facets.

We often talk about the Balkans like it's some mysterious culture that vanished long ago. Myths and legends make these lands seem mystical.

The very concept of the 'Balkans' is controversial: there are numerous contradictory definitions of the region, sometimes geographical and sometimes ideological. When we discuss the Balkans, we are speaking about an area surrounded by four seas: the Black Sea, the Aegean Sea, the Ionian Sea and the Adriatic Sea, and of two vast empires that conquered many territories, spreading their culture: the Byzantine Empire of Constantinople, and the Ottoman Empire of Istanbul.

The territories in question have witnessed a procession of people through the centuries – countless travellers, occupiers from distant lands and waves of migrants in search of a better life. The Balkans play a unique role geographically. They are, in a way, the natural border between the East and the West. They not only connect two large geographical areas, but two great cultures. From this blend, a curious culinary mix was born, with similar dishes found across countries, sometimes under different names, their ingredients varying, but with common roots and techniques.

Instead of engaging in scholarly disputes over the exact borders of the Balkans, I chose to opt for a more personal interpretation: one that is rooted in my experience of a common shared identity. I discovered this identity in the artistic craftsmanship of the peoples in question, and in culinary traditions, which have shaped my belief that the Balkans stretch from Greece to Hungary in the west, and from Türkiye to Moldova in the east. Although this definition is a very personal one, it has allowed me to share my heritage and the innumerable culinary riches in this part of the world – so don't be surprised to discover dishes as diverse as Korean-style marinated cabbage, schnitzels like you'd find in Austria, tahini like in Lebanon, molasses like in Türkiye and coffee like in Tunisia!

I invite you to travel through these lands that, shaped by mighty empires, have merged the best of the West and the best of the East into their own cuisine.

This rich culinary heritage is derived from the presence of four fundamental elements:

Water. The Balkans are surrounded by four seas full of diverse seafood that forms an integral part of our cuisine.

Fire. Due to the abundance of forest and mountains, our people have developed a culture of wood, fire and barbecue, with wood-fired cookers giving

an unrivalled aroma to our food. It's not summer without an open fire cooking a huge piece of meat and some freshly picked seasonal vegetables.

Earth. Before anything, we are farmers or descendants of farmers. In many Balkan families, there is a home in the country where grandparents and perhaps great-grandparents still live, working small fields. We are a people accustomed to having our hands in the dirt, to planting crops in spring and summer and taking livestock out to pasture across the seasons.

Climate. The expanse of our lands brings quite a wide-ranging climate, which has made us very creative in the kitchen! From very hot summers, with fruit and vegetables in abundance, we move into frigid winters. To face the winter months, we developed the custom of stockpiling vegetables by canning and preserving them, using salt and smoke to keep meats for as long as possible.

This cookbook aims to immerse you in our traditions and unique culture, to take you on a journey through the culinary heritage of a people undoubtedly hardened by adversity, but who are still warm and welcoming.

In a world which is rapidly changing, and in which we no longer take the time to question the way we live and consume, it seemed useful to me to return to the sources of our humanity, and what makes us unique as human beings.

We acquire our individuality through our experiences and our memories, which often begin around a table. Much more than just an object, this table is a symbol of family, of sharing, of connection, of nostalgia, of inheritance and of carrying on traditions.

It's this heritage that I want to share with you through this collection of recipes that I think are most representative of our culture. They are also the ones I most enjoy cooking for my own children, reminding them of their dual cultures, with the hope that they, in turn, will want to express themselves through the joys of a wonderful meal.

RECIPE LEGEND

❋

Vegetarian

🌾

Gluten-free

I use fan-forced oven temperatures for the recipes in this book. If you have a conventional oven, simply increase the temperature by 20°C (70°F).

IBRIK

Noun

A traditional copper pot used
to prepare Turkish coffee, found
in kitchens across the Balkans.

MEZZE

MEZZE IS A HAPPY EXCUSE FOR SHARING A MOMENT TOGETHER. WHETHER THE DISHES ARE SERVED SIMPLY AS A SNACK, OR AS STARTERS FOR A MULTI-COURSE MEAL, WHAT COUNTS IS ABUNDANCE AND NOT NECESSARILY COMPLEXITY.

On the table, you might find dolmades and eggplant 'caviar' alongside cheese or sliced smoked meats, and your hosts will bring out the best of what they have in their pantry. Wherever you go in the Balkans, you will find the same traditions – a generously laden table is a sign of abundance, wealth and hospitality.

WHITE BEAN DIP

SERVES 6

250 g (1¼ cups) dried white beans, such as tarbais or haricot
2 carrots, roughly chopped
¼ celeriac, roughly chopped
4 garlic cloves, crushed
70 ml (2¼ fl oz) sunflower oil
finely sliced spring onion (scallion), to garnish (optional)
Pita bread (page 154), to serve (optional; omit to keep recipe gluten free)

Onion sauce

40 ml (1¼ fl oz) sunflower oil
2 onions, diced
pinch of salt
50 g (1¾ oz) tomato paste (concentrated puree)
1 garlic clove, grated

Place the white beans in a large bowl. Pour in 1 litre (4 cups) of cold water, cover with plastic wrap and leave overnight in the fridge.

The next day, drain the beans, then place in a large saucepan with plenty of cold water. Add the carrot and celeriac, but do not salt. Bring to the boil, then reduce to a simmer and cook for about 2 hours, until the beans are tender. Let rest for 1 hour.

Drain the beans, retaining 350 ml (12 fl oz) of the broth. Discard the carrot and celeriac.

Place the cooked beans in a blender or food processor with the garlic. With the motor running, slowly drizzle in the sunflower oil. If the mixture is too thick, drizzle in the reserved broth until it is smooth and the consistency of hummus. Season to taste with salt.

Transfer to a bowl, cover and place in the fridge for at least 30 minutes to thicken.

To make the onion sauce, heat the sunflower oil in a pan over low heat. Add the onion and season with the salt and pepper. Cook, stirring now and then, until the onion is caramelised. Stir in the tomato paste and garlic and cook for another 5 minutes, then leave to cool.

Serve the dip drizzled with the onion sauce. If desired, garnish with spring onion and enjoy with a side of pita bread.

Note: *You can roast the garlic in the oven before adding it.*

CHICKPEA HUMMUS

SERVES 6

200 g (7 oz) dried chickpeas (garbanzo beans)
75 ml (2½ fl oz) sunflower oil
20 ml (¾ fl oz) lemon juice
2 garlic cloves, crushed
1 tablespoon tahini
¾ teaspoon ground cumin

To serve

1 teaspoon Espelette chilli powder or chilli powder
3 parsley sprigs, chopped
pine nuts
roast vegetables (optional)

Place the chickpeas in a large bowl. Pour in 1 litre (4 cups) of cold water, cover with plastic wrap and leave overnight in the fridge.

The next day, drain the chickpeas, then place in a large saucepan with plenty of cold water. Bring to the boil, then reduce to a simmer and cook for 2 hours, or until the chickpeas are tender.

Drain the chickpeas, reserving 75 ml (2½ fl oz) of the cooking water.

Transfer the cooked chickpeas to a blender or food processor. Add the sunflower oil, lemon juice, garlic, tahini, cumin and salt, then puree for 7–10 minutes. Gradually add small amounts of the cooking water until smooth.

Serve the hummus sprinkled with the chilli powder, parsley and pine nuts. If desired, top with roast vegetables, such as cauliflower.

Note: *For an even smoother, creamier hummus, remove the skin of the cooked chickpeas before blending by rubbing them between your hands with a clean tea towel.*

EGGPLANT 'CAVIAR' WITH CARAMEL

SERVES 6

5 firm, shiny eggplants (aubergines)
75–85 ml (2½–2¾ fl oz) sunflower oil
1¾ teaspoons fine salt
1 teaspoon granulated sugar
1 red onion, diced
Pita bread (page 154), to serve
  (optional; omit to keep
  recipe gluten free)

Poke holes into the eggplants with a wooden toothpick.

Grill the eggplants in a chargrill pan over medium–high heat (or in an oven set to 230°C/450°F) until the skin is charred and the flesh is tender, making sure to turn them regularly.

Place the grilled eggplants in a bowl, cover with plastic wrap, then leave at room temperature for 30 minutes.

Remove the skin from the eggplants and discard. Place the flesh in a strainer set over a bowl and let drain for at least 2 hours, to collect the cooking juices.

Place the drained eggplants on a wooden board and finely chop them using a non-metallic spatula.

Transfer to a bowl. While stirring vigorously, gradually add the sunflower oil and salt.

To make the caramel, place 50 ml (1¾ fl oz) of the reserved eggplant cooking juices in a saucepan with the sugar. Bring to the boil, then simmer over low heat for 6–8 minutes until the mixture darkens and becomes syrupy.

Drizzle the caramel over the eggplant 'caviar' and top with the red onion. If desired, serve with pita bread on the side.

EGGPLANT WITH NETTLE SAUCE

SERVES 6

6 small eggplants (aubergines), halved
  lengthways
50 ml (1¾ fl oz) olive oil
3 garlic cloves, chopped
2 tablespoons molasses
1 tablespoon apple cider vinegar
1 tablespoon honey
toasted pumpkin seeds, to garnish

Nettle sauce

150 g (5½ oz) nettles (see Note
  on page 105) (or spinach/chard)
pinch of salt
40 ml (1¼ fl oz) olive oil
100 ml (3½ fl oz) cream
2 shallots, sliced
2 garlic cloves, minced
1 sprig of thyme
1 bay leaf

Preheat the oven to 160°C (320°F).

Place the eggplant halves, cut side up, on a baking tray. Use a sharp knife to deeply score the flesh in a diagonal checkerboard pattern.

In a bowl, mix together the olive oil, garlic, molasses, vinegar and honey. Season with salt and pepper. Brush the mixture over the eggplants and bake for 45 minutes.

To make the nettle sauce, put on a pair of gloves and pick the leaves from the nettles, removing any large stems and damaged leaves. Rinse the leaves in plenty of water two or three times.

In a saucepan, add 1.5 litres (6 cups) of water with the salt and bring to the boil. Add the nettles, reduce to a simmer and leave to

cook for 15 minutes. Scoop the nettles out using a slotted spoon and immerse them in a bowl of cold water. Set aside.

Place the remaining sauce ingredients in a frying pan over medium heat. Season with salt and pepper and cook for a few minutes, until the shallot turns slightly white. Add the nettles and cook for about 15 minutes, until the shallot has browned and the nettles have wilted. Remove the bay leaf and thyme.

Transfer the sauce to a blender or food processor and blend briefly until smooth and creamy.

Serve the eggplants drizzled with the sauce and sprinkled with a few toasted pumpkin seeds.

CRUMBED ZUCCHINI

SERVES 6

300 g (10½ oz) zucchinis (courgettes), cut into half-moons

200 g (7 oz) stale bread, chopped into small pieces

200 g (1⅓ cups) plain (all-purpose) flour

2 eggs

1 litre (4 cups) grapeseed oil

mint leaves, to serve (optional)

✽

Lightly salt the zucchini on all sides. Place on a tray and refrigerate for 5 minutes, then gently wipe off any excess moisture.

Using a blender, blitz the bread into a fairly fine powder.

Place the breadcrumbs and flour in two separate bowls. Beat the eggs in a third bowl. Gently dip the zucchini pieces in the flour, then the egg, and finally in the breadcrumbs.

In a saucepan with sides deep enough to avoid risk of splashing or boiling over, heat the grapeseed oil to 180°C (350°F), or until

a cube of bread dropped in the oil browns in 15 seconds. Using a skimmer, immerse the zucchini in the oil and fry for about 2 minutes, until golden.

Remove the zucchini using the skimmer and drain on paper towel, then season with more salt, if desired.

Serve immediately, with ktipiti (below) or tzatziki (page 22). It is also lovely with some pickled red onion (page 136) and mint leaves on the side.

KTIPITI

SERVES 6

½ fresh spicy long green chilli, roughly chopped

200 g (7 oz) Greek-style yoghurt

200 g (7 oz) feta, chopped

75 ml (2½ fl oz) olive oil

✽ 🌿

Generally, this recipe is made with red chilli, but I personally prefer this version, which is enjoyed in the villages of northern Greece.

Using a mortar and pestle, crush the green chilli into a paste.

In a small bowl, mix together the yoghurt, feta and olive oil by hand, or with a blender on low speed.

Gradually add the chilli to the mixture until you reach your desired level of spiciness.

Season with salt if needed.

The ktipiti is delicious with dishes such as chicken souvlaki (page 118) and tzatziki (page 22).

CRUMBED CALAMARI AND ANCHOVIES

SERVES 6

250 g (9 oz) cleaned fresh squid
250 g (9 oz) fresh anchovies, gutted
  and cleaned
300 g (2 cups) plain (all-purpose) flour
200 g (7 oz) fine polenta or cornmeal
2 eggs
1 litre (4 cups) grapeseed oil
chopped parsley, to serve
1 lemon, halved, to serve

Garlic sauce

100 ml (3½ fl oz) milk
1 garlic clove
3 pinches of salt
250 ml (1 cup) grapeseed oil

To make the garlic sauce, heat the milk in a saucepan with the garlic clove and salt over low heat for 5–7 minutes, until warm, to infuse the milk. Pour the mixture into a food processor and blend in the grapeseed oil until you have a mayonnaise consistency. Transfer the garlic sauce to a small bowl for serving.

Cut the squid into rings and keep the anchovies whole. Place the seafood on a plate and store in the fridge.

Place the flour and polenta in two separate bowls. Beat the eggs in a third bowl. Dip the squid rings in the flour, then the egg and finally in the polenta. Coat the anchovies only in the polenta and store in the fridge until ready for frying.

In a saucepan with sides deep enough to avoid risk of splashing or boiling over, heat the grapeseed oil to 180°C (350°F), or until a cube of bread dropped in the oil browns in 15 seconds.

Fry the squid rings first, gently dropping them into the oil and cooking for 3–5 minutes, until golden and tender. Remove with a slotted spoon onto paper towel, then season with salt. Repeat with the anchovies, cooking them for only 2 minutes.

Serve the hot fried calamari and anchovies on a platter, sprinkled with chopped parsley, with the garlic sauce and lemon halves on the side.

Note: *If you can't find fresh anchovies, you can use other small fish such as smelt or whitebait.*

TZATZIKI

SERVES 6

500 g (2 cups) Greek-style yoghurt
85 g (3 oz) cucumber
1 garlic clove
juice of ½ lemon
2 teaspoons olive oil
dill sprigs, to garnish (optional)
Cornbread (page 158), to serve
  (optional; omit to keep
  recipe gluten free)

Line a colander with muslin (cheesecloth) or a clean thin tea towel. Place the colander over a bowl, pour the yoghurt into it and cover. Let the yoghurt drain in the fridge overnight to remove the excess liquid.

The next day, finely grate the cucumber. Place the grated cucumber on a clean tea towel and sprinkle with sea salt to speed up the release of excess water – this will take 10–15 minutes. Squeeze the cloth tightly to remove as much liquid as possible.

Grate the garlic into a bowl. Add the grated cucumber, drained yoghurt, lemon juice and olive oil, stirring to combine. Season to taste with salt and pepper.

If desired, you can serve garnished with a few dill sprigs and a grind of pepper, with cornbread on the side.

Note: *This mezze pairs perfectly with most of the recipes in this book – that's its little secret! To enhance the tzatziki's texture and freshness, you can top with diced cucumber just before serving.*

COLESLAW WITH YOGHURT

SERVES 6

125 g (½ cup) Greek-style yoghurt
100 g (3½ oz) carrots, grated
500 g (1 lb 2 oz) white cabbage,
  finely sliced
3 spring onions (scallions),
  finely chopped
1 granny smith apple
juice of 1 lemon
pinch of salt
50 g (⅓ cup) cashews
1 pomegranate

Mayonnaise

2 hard-boiled eggs, peeled
1 egg yolk
1 teaspoon salt
230 ml (8 fl oz) sunflower oil
30 ml (1 fl oz) sparkling water
juice of ½ lemon
1 tablespoon dijon mustard

To make the mayonnaise, remove the yolks from the hard-boiled eggs and pass them through a sieve, into a bowl. Add the raw egg yolk and salt and mix until well combined. Slowly pour in the sunflower oil, 1 tablespoon at a time, whisking continuously. Occasionally add a few drops of the sparkling water to dilute the mayonnaise and for a smoother texture. Once whipped, stir in the lemon juice and mustard and season to taste with salt and pepper.

Mix 30 g (1 oz) of the mayonnaise through the yoghurt and season with salt and pepper. The remaining mayonnaise can be stored in an airtight container in the fridge for up to 24 hours.

Preheat the oven to 160°C (320°F).

In a large bowl, toss together the carrot, cabbage and spring onion. Cut the apple into julienne strips, add to the bowl and sprinkle with the lemon juice. Mix the yoghurt dressing through the coleslaw with the salt, then cover and chill for 30 minutes in the fridge.

Meanwhile, roast the cashews in the oven for 10 minutes. Leave to cool, then roughly chop or crush them in a mortar.

Cut the pomegranate in half and lightly tap the skin with a spatula over a bowl to extract the seeds. Remove any remaining white membrane from the seeds, as it is bitter.

Serve the coleslaw sprinkled with the pomegranate seeds and roasted cashews.

Note: *Remember to always roast your nuts – their flavour will be increased ten-fold.*

ZACUSCĂ

SERVES 6

1.5 kg (3 lb 5 oz) eggplants
  (aubergines)
1 kg (2 lb 3 oz) red bell peppers
  (capsicums)
300 g (10½ oz) onions, halved
60 ml (¼ cup) sunflower oil
2 garlic cloves, minced
¼ teaspoon coriander seeds
½ teaspoon black peppercorns
3 bay leaves
1 thyme sprig
1 tablespoon tomato paste
  (concentrated puree)
210 g (7½ oz) tinned finely
  chopped tomatoes

On a barbecue (or in a chargrill pan on the stove), grill the eggplants, bell peppers and onions over direct high heat until their skins are charred and the flesh is tender, making sure to turn them regularly. Transfer the grilled vegetables to a deep dish, cover with plastic wrap and leave at room temperature for 30 minutes.

Once the vegetables have cooled, remove the skins and stalks from the eggplants, and the skins, stalks and seeds from the bell peppers. Finely chop the flesh of all the grilled vegetables.

Heat the sunflower oil in a saucepan over high heat.

Add the grilled vegetables, garlic, coriander, peppercorns, bay leaves and thyme sprig and saute for 5 minutes. Reduce the heat to low and cook for another 15 minutes.

Stir in the tomato paste and chopped tomatoes, then simmer over low heat for 45 minutes. Season with salt and pepper.

Enjoy the zacuscă served like a regular tomato relish.

It will keep in a sterilised airtight jar fitted with a rubber seal for up to 3 weeks unopened.

GRILLED BELL PEPPERS WITH FETA

SERVES 6

12 red bell peppers (capsicums)
250 g (9 oz) feta
1 handful of buckwheat groats
½ bunch of dill, sprigs picked
70 ml (2¼ fl oz) olive oil

Marinade

600 ml (20½ fl oz) olive oil
200 ml (7 fl oz) apple cider vinegar
10 garlic cloves, crushed
4 thyme sprigs
2 bay leaves
2 tablespoons black peppercorns
2 tablespoons timut peppercorns or
  Sichuan peppercorns

Grill the bell peppers on a barbecue (or in a chargrill pan on the stove) over direct high heat until the skin is charred, making sure to turn them regularly.

Transfer the bell peppers to a deep dish, cover with plastic wrap and leave at room temperature for 30 minutes.

Once they have cooled, carefully remove the skins, stalks and seeds, without damaging the flesh.

Place all the marinade ingredients in a large bowl and mix until combined. Add the peeled bell peppers, cover with plastic wrap and refrigerate for at least 3 hours, or overnight for even more flavour.

To serve, arrange the marinated bell peppers on a plate and crumble the feta over top. Sprinkle with the buckwheat groats and dill sprigs, season with salt and finish with the olive oil.

VILLAGE SALAD

SERVES 6

6 large ripe heirloom tomatoes
½ bell pepper (capsicum) (red, green
  or a mix)
½ red onion
½ cucumber, or 3 small dill pickles
  (gherkins)
300 g (10½ oz) feta, sliced
150 g (5½ oz) kalamata olives, pitted
thyme or oregano sprigs, to garnish

Vinaigrette

2 tablespoons olive oil
75 ml (2¾ fl oz) apple cider vinegar
1 tablespoon honey
fresh or dried oregano, to taste

Using a mandoline or very sharp knife, thinly slice the tomatoes, bell pepper, onion and cucumber. Arrange the slices on a serving dish or in a wide shallow bowl.

Arrange the feta on top of the salad and scatter the olives around.

Place the vinaigrette ingredients in a bowl, season with salt and pepper and mix vigorously until combined.

Pour the vinaigrette over the salad. Serve garnished with thyme or oregano.

Notes: *This salad – a staple of the Greek diet in summer – is wonderful with any barbecued meat, especially chicken souvlaki (page 118) or beef souvlaki.*

If you have some bread on hand that's starting to go stale, simply toast it in the oven for a few minutes. It will go perfectly with this salad.

MEZZE

SPINACH AND FETA BÖREK

SERVES 6

Filo pastry

275 g (9½ oz) plain (all-purpose) flour
175 g (6 oz) softened butter
1 egg
1 teaspoon apple cider vinegar
1 teaspoon lemon juice
1 teaspoon salt
cornflour (corn starch), for dusting
100 g (3½ oz) butter, melted

Filling

50 ml (1¾ fl oz) olive oil
1 red onion, finely chopped
2 spring onions (scallions),
  finely chopped
3 garlic cloves, crushed
2 thyme sprigs
800 g (1 lb 12 oz) spinach leaves,
  chopped
250 g (9 oz) feta
2 eggs

❋

IBRIK

To make the filo pastry, place the flour, butter, egg, vinegar, lemon juice and salt in a bowl. Mix in 85 ml (2¾ fl oz) of water and stir until combined.

In the bowl, knead the dough for 10 minutes, until smooth, then form into a ball. Cover with a damp tea towel and let rest for 20 minutes at room temperature.

Meanwhile, make the filling. Heat the olive oil in a frying pan over high heat, then saute the onion, spring onion, garlic and thyme for 5 minutes. Transfer to a bowl, discarding the thyme sprigs.

In the same pan, cook the spinach over medium heat for 1–2 minutes, then add to the sauteed onion mixture. Crumble the feta into the bowl, crack in the eggs and mix well. Season to taste with salt and pepper and set to the side.

Divide the dough into two equal pieces. Shape each piece into a log, then cut each log into 10 even pieces. Roll each piece into a ball, place on a baking tray and cover with a damp tea towel.

On a work surface lightly dusted with cornflour, work with one piece of dough at a time, keeping the rest covered. Roll out each ball of dough with a rolling pin until the dough is as thin as possible; you should be able to see through it. Place on a plate, sprinkling each sheet with a little cornflour to stop them sticking together, and cover with a damp tea towel.

Preheat the oven to 180°C (350°F).

Use some of the melted butter to brush the bottom and sides of the pan. Place a sheet of filo pastry on the bottom of the pan and brush with some of the melted butter. Place a second sheet on top and brush with more butter. Repeat this process until you have 10 sheets of dough layered.

Using a spatula, spread the filling over the layered filo sheets, then cover with 10 more layers of pastry, buttering each pastry layer as you go.

Transfer to the oven and bake for 30 minutes, until the pastry is golden.

Rest the börek for 5–10 minutes before serving.

Note: *If you would like to use store-bought filo pastry, make sure it is good quality and that the sheets are very thin.*

GRILLED SARDINES

SERVES 6

18 small fresh sardines, gutted

1 lemon, sliced

Marinade

300 ml (10 fl oz) olive oil

2–3 rosemary sprigs

2–3 thyme sprigs

4 garlic cloves, crushed

zest and juice of 1 lemon

2 shallots, chopped

4 pinches of sea salt

To serve

1 lemon, finely diced

½ bunch of chives, chopped

30 g (1 oz) salted roasted pistachios, roughly chopped

2 pinches of ground sumac

To make the marinade, place 200 ml (7 fl oz) of the olive oil in a heatproof bowl with the rosemary, thyme and two garlic cloves. Pour the remaining 100 ml (3½ fl oz) of the olive oil into a small saucepan and heat to 90°C (195°F), or until small bubbles form around the handle of a wooden spoon dipped in the oil. Pour the hot oil over the cold oil mixture, then leave to infuse at room temperature until completely cool.

Remove the herbs and garlic from the cooled oil. Add the remaining two garlic cloves, along with the remaining marinade ingredients.

In a shallow glass dish, layer the sardines and lemon slices and drizzle generously with the marinade. Cover with plastic wrap and marinate in the fridge for 30 minutes.

When ready to serve, remove the sardines from the marinade and sear in a very hot cast-iron skillet or frying pan for 2 minutes on each side.

Line the grilled sardines on a large plate and serve sprinkled with the lemon, chives, pistachios and sumac.

ROAST BEEF WITH OLIVIER SALAD

SERVES 6

500 g (1 lb 2 oz) roast beef (or a small
   roast beef)

½ tablespoon olive oil

4 garlic cloves, crushed

2 thyme sprigs

dill sprigs, to garnish

Olivier salad

½ celeriac

500 g (1 lb 2 oz) baby potatoes, peeled

3 large carrots, peeled

300 g (10½ oz) peas (preferably fresh
   podded peas)

1 small tart apple

3 large sweet and sour dill pickles
   (gherkins)

4–6 tablespoons Mayonnaise (page 25)

This dish is often enjoyed
during the holidays. It has
its origins in Russia, where
it was named Olivier salad
after the Belgian chef who
invented it.

Bring the beef to room temperature before cooking, to avoid thermal shock and for the most tender result.

Preheat the oven to 210°C (410°F).

Heat the olive oil in a large saucepan over high heat. Sear the beef until browned on all sides. Season with sea salt, then transfer to a baking dish. Add the garlic and thyme sprigs. (Leave the beef cooking juices in the saucepan for now.)

Roast the beef for 10–15 minutes; it is ready when the juices run pink and the internal temperature reaches 50–55°C (120–130°F) when tested with a meat thermometer. Remove from the oven and discard the garlic and thyme. Season with pepper, cover with foil and set aside to rest.

While the beef is resting, prepare the salad. Pour a little water into the saucepan you used to brown the beef and place back over high heat. Scrape the bottom of the pan with a spatula to loosen any solids and cooking juices. Add the celeriac to the pan and about 500–750 ml (2–3 cups) of water – enough to poach the salad vegetables.

Bring to the boil, then add the celeriac and cook for 15 minutes, skimming regularly as soon as any brown foam appears on the surface of the broth. Add the potatoes and carrots and cook for another 15 minutes, or until the potatoes are tender but the carrots are still a little firm when pierced with a fork or the tip of a knife. Remove the potatoes and carrots from the broth and set aside.

Poach the peas in the boiling broth for 5 minutes, or until just tender. Drain the peas, discarding the celeriac and broth. (The celeriac was only used for flavouring the broth.)

Finely dice the potatoes, carrots, apple and pickles, so they are all about the same size as the peas. Place them in a salad bowl with the peas. Add 4 tablespoons of the mayonnaise and gently mix together with a spatula, adding more mayonnaise if needed to bind the ingredients.

Divide the salad among serving plates. Add the roast beef, thinly sliced and rolled for serving, and garnish with dill.

TANGY BEETROOT SALAD

SERVES 6

4 beetroot (beets)
olive oil, for brushing
1 pink lady apple, peeled
juice of 1 lemon
chopped spring onion (scallion),
  to garnish
chopped parsley, to garnish

Dressing
1 tablespoon honey
1 tablespoon apple cider vinegar
50 ml (1¾ fl oz) olive oil

Preheat the oven to 200°C (400°F).

Place each beetroot on a separate piece of foil. Brush with olive oil and season with salt and pepper. Wrap into individual parcels and place on a baking tray.

Bake the beetroot for 45 minutes, or until the centres are tender when pierced with a fork or the tip of a knife.

Remove from the oven, leave them wrapped in foil and rest at room temperature for 30 minutes. Once cooled, remove the foil. Peel the beetroot, then thinly slice using a mandoline or very sharp knife. Place the slices in a salad bowl, cover and chill in the fridge until needed.

To make the dressing, mix the honey and vinegar in a small bowl and season with salt and pepper. Slowly whisk in the olive oil until smooth and emulsified.

Drizzle the dressing over the beetroot. Cut the apple into julienne strips and arrange on top, then squeeze the lemon juice over. Garnish with spring onion and parsley and serve.

Note: *You can also roast the beetroot in coarse salt. Avoid using the vacuum-packed beetroot sold in supermarkets, as the salad won't be as flavoursome.*

LABNEH WITH BUTTERNUT PUMPKIN

SERVES 6

¼ red kuri or butternut
  pumpkin (squash)
50 g (1¾ oz) honey
2 tablespoons olive oil
1 garlic clove, crushed
1 tablespoon sweet paprika
1 tablespoon ground cumin
1 teaspoon za'atar

Labneh

200 g (7 oz) Greek-style yoghurt
juice of ½ lemon
olive oil, for drizzling

To serve

vine leaves in brine or mint
finely chopped chives
crushed pistachios
Koulouri (page 161; omit to keep
  recipe gluten free)

✳ ❧

Labneh can be made in a
variety of delicious ways.
Here, I've chosen the
method that's easiest
to do at home.

If serving with vine leaves, preheat the oven to 65°C (150°F).

Pat the leaves dry and spread in a single layer over a baking tray, then bake with the oven door left ajar for at least 1 hour, until crisp, checking them every 15 minutes.

Remove from the oven and allow to cool, then transfer to an airtight container and store in your pantry.

Meanwhile, prepare the labneh. Line a colander with muslin (cheesecloth) or a clean thin tea towel. Place the colander over a bowl, pour the yoghurt into it and cover. Let the yoghurt drain in the fridge overnight to remove the excess liquid.

The next day, pour the drained yogurt into a bowl, then add the lemon juice and a drizzle of olive oil. Mix and season to taste with salt, then cover and store in the fridge until ready to serve.

Preheat the oven to 180°C (350°F).

Cut the pumpkin into 5 cm (2 in) cubes (see Notes) and place in a bowl. Add the honey, olive oil, garlic, paprika and cumin and mix well to coat all the pumpkin.

Spread the coated pumpkin over a baking tray and bake for 30 minutes, until the pumpkin is soft in the centre when pierced with a fork or the tip of a knife.

Remove the pumpkin from the baking tray, then carefully tip any cooking juices into a small bowl. Mix the za'atar into the reserved pumpkin juices, adding a little olive oil if you need more liquid.

To serve, spread the labneh on a plate, make a well in the centre and arrange the roasted pumpkin on top. Drizzle with the za'atar mixture and finish with chives, vine or mint leaves, and pistachios. If desired, enjoy with koulouri.

Notes: *The pumpkin doesn't need to be peeled for this dish as it has a very thin skin that becomes tender when roasted, but you can of course peel it if you prefer.*

Use any left-over vine leaves to serve with dishes of your choice.

DOLMADES WITH SOUR CHERRIES

SERVES 6

800 ml (27 fl oz) vegetable or
chicken stock (or water)
40 vine leaves in brine
120 ml (4 fl oz) olive oil
juice of 1 lemon
40 sour cherries, halved
chopped dill, to serve

Filling

1 tablespoon olive oil
2 small onions, diced
200 g (1 cup) short-grain white rice
zest of 1 lemon
1 bunch of dill, finely chopped
1 garlic clove, finely grated
1 tablespoon ground fennel seeds

I was given this recipe by
a Greek yiayia who is very
dear to me. Her secret,
I think, is the generous
amount of dill that flavours
the rice. The more dill, the
better the dolmades!

To make the filling, heat the olive oil in a frying pan over low heat and gently cook the onion for a few minutes, until soft and transparent. Add the rice and stir constantly for 2–3 minutes, until the rice is translucent.

Add the lemon zest, dill, garlic, fennel and a ladleful of the stock. Gradually pour in another 300 ml (10 fl oz) of the stock and bring to the boil. Reduce the heat to low, cover and continue to cook until the liquid is completely absorbed. Season to taste with salt and pepper, then remove from the heat and leave to cool.

Preheat the oven to 170°C (340°F).

Remove the vine leaves from their jar, carefully wash them one by one, and dry them with paper towel.

To make the dolmades, place a vine leaf on a work surface, central vein facing up, and cut off the stem. Place 1 tablespoon of the cooled filling at the bottom of the leaf. Fold the left and right sides of the leaf over the filling, then roll up from the bottom to the tip. Repeat to make more dolmades, until you have used up all the filling. Reserve the remaining vine leaves.

Line a deep baking dish with three layers of vine leaves (to help protect the dolmades). Arrange the dolmades tightly together in the dish, overlapping them if necessary. Drizzle with the remaining broth, olive oil and lemon juice, then add the cherries. Arrange the remaining vine leaves over the top, then cover with foil and bake for 30–40 minutes, until the rice is tender.

Serve the dolmades, hot or cold, with dill and the sour cherries.

Note: *The smaller the dolmades, the more flavourful they are. Be sure to pack the rolls firmly so they don't unfurl during cooking.*

RUSTIC PITA SCROLLS WITH FETA

SERVES 6

Dough

25 g (1 oz) fresh yeast
1 tablespoon fine semolina
370 g (13 oz) plain (all-purpose) flour,
  plus extra for dusting
1 tablespoon granulated sugar
50 ml (1¾ fl oz) sunflower oil, plus
  extra for greasing
1 teaspoon vinegar
1 teaspoon salt

Filling

250 g (9 oz) feta cheese, grated
250 g (1 cup) cream cheese
100 g (3½ oz) kalamata olives,
  quartered
1 bunch of dill, chopped
1 red onion, diced
2 spring onions (scallions), diced
50 ml (1¾ fl oz) olive oil

Glaze

1 egg yolk
1 tablespoon milk

✳

To make the dough, place the yeast, semolina and 1 level tablespoon of the flour in a large bowl. Add 150 ml (5 fl oz) of lukewarm water and mix using a wooden spoon. Leave to sit for 15 minutes, until the yeast is bubbly.

Stir in the sugar, sunflower oil, vinegar and salt. Sift the remaining flour over the top and mix until the dough forms a ball.

Oil your hands and work surface. Tip the dough out of the bowl and knead it for about 10 minutes, until it becomes elastic.

Now continue to knead the dough vigorously with the palm of your hand for another 20 minutes or so, until it is smooth and no longer sticky.

Place the dough in a floured bowl and cover with plastic wrap. Leave to rise at warm room temperature (around 25°C/77°F) for 45 minutes, until doubled in size.

While the dough is proving, combine all the filling ingredients in a bowl. Season with salt and pepper and mix until smooth. Cover and refrigerate until needed.

To make the pita scrolls, preheat the oven to 180°C (350°F). Line a baking tray with baking paper.

Use about 100 ml (3½ fl oz) of sunflower oil to coat your hands, work surface and rolling pin.

Knead the dough again with the palm of your hand to deflate it. Cut the dough into six equal pieces and form into balls.

Place a ball of dough on the oiled work surface. Using your rolling pin, roll the dough out to a diameter of about 15 cm (6 in). Oil the dough any time it becomes crumbly. Finish rolling out the dough by hand to a diameter of about 20 cm (8 in). Using a spoon, roughly spread one-sixth of the filling over the dough, leaving a thin margin (about 1 cm/½ in) around the edge. Starting from the bottom edge, roll the dough, pressing tightly, to form a long roll. Twist the roll like a rope, then coil the rope into a scroll shape.

Repeat to make another five pita scrolls, placing them on the lined baking tray. In a small bowl, whisk the glaze ingredients, then brush the glaze over the scrolls.

Bake for about 25 minutes, until the pastry is beautifully golden.

Best enjoyed warm from the oven.

Note: *Change the filling to suit your tastes! You can also make a delicious sweet pita by adding 2 more tablespoons of sugar to the dough and using a fruit filling – apples, pears and dried fruits all work well.*

BEEF AND HERB KOFTAS

SERVES 6

100 g (1 cup) fine dried breadcrumbs
2 eggs
1 litre (4 cups) grapeseed oil
chopped parsley and dill, to serve
Pita bread (page 154), to serve

Kofta

20 g (¾ oz) stale bread
50 ml (1¾ fl oz) sunflower oil
2 onions, grated
250 g (9 oz) carrots, peeled and grated
1 large potato, peeled and grated
500 g (1 lb 2 oz) minced (ground) beef
1 egg
4 garlic cloves, grated
1 bunch of dill, chopped
1 bunch of parsley, chopped
2 teaspoons fine salt
1 teaspoon smoked paprika
1 teaspoon ground black pepper

Lovage sauce

250 g (1 cup) Greek-style yoghurt
40 ml (1¼ fl oz) sunflower oil
½ bunch of lovage
juice of 1 lemon

To make the kofta, place the bread in a bowl. Fill with water, cover and leave to soak in the fridge for 10–15 minutes, until softened.

Heat the sunflower oil in a frying pan and saute the onion over medium heat for a few minutes, until soft and translucent. Add the carrot and potato and saute for 3–4 minutes, until tender. Let cool.

Place the beef in a large bowl with the remaining kofta ingredients and cooled sauteed vegetables.

Drain the bread in-between your hands. Add it to the bowl and mix everything by hand for at least 10 minutes, until smooth and fluffy. Cover with plastic wrap and rest in the fridge for 30 minutes.

Combine the sauce ingredients with a pinch of salt in a blender and whiz until smooth. Adjust the seasoning to taste.

When ready to cook the kofta, place the breadcrumbs in a bowl. Beat the eggs in a second bowl.

Using your hands, form the kofta mixture into meatballs, using about 100 g (3½ oz) for each. Flatten slightly into ovals.

Dip the koftas in the egg, then the breadcrumbs, making sure they are evenly coated. Transfer to the fridge until ready to fry.

In a saucepan with sides deep enough to avoid splashing or boiling over, heat the oil to 180°C (350°F), or until a cube of bread in the oil browns in 15 seconds. Fry the koftas for 5–6 minutes, until golden brown. Remove with a slotted spoon, drain on paper towel and season with salt.

Serve warm, drizzled with sauce. If desired, sprinkle with parsley and dill and serve with pita bread.

TABOULEH

SERVES 6

150 g (5½ oz) burghul
1 thyme sprig
1 bay leaf
2 bunches of parsley, chopped
4 spring onions (scallions), chopped
4 garlic cloves
200 g (7 oz) sun-dried tomatoes
100 ml (3½ fl oz) olive oil
60 ml (¼ cup) pomegranate molasses
½ pomegranate
1 bunch of mint, chopped
ground sumac, for sprinkling

Bring a saucepan of salted water to the boil. Cook the burghul according to the packet instructions, adding the thyme and bay leaf to the cooking water. Drain the burghul thoroughly, transfer to a large bowl and leave to cool. Cover with plastic wrap and refrigerate until cold.

Place the parsley, spring onion and garlic in a food processor with the sun-dried tomatoes, olive oil and pomegranate molasses. Season with a little sea salt. Pulse until

the mixture is roughly chopped and smooth, but not mushy. Add the parsley mixture to the burghul and mix together.

Extract the seeds from the pomegranate by tapping it on its skin with a spatula. Remove any remaining white membrane from the seeds, as it is bitter.

Sprinkle the pomegranate seeds and mint over the tabouleh. Season to taste with salt, pepper and sumac.

GRILLED HALLOUMI WITH CANDIED LEMON ZEST

SERVES 6

3 lemons
125 g (4½ oz) granulated sugar
pinch of salt
450 g (1 lb) halloumi, cut into 1 cm
  (½ in) thick slices
20 ml (¾ fl oz) olive oil
1 tablespoon honey

❋ ⚘

Halloumi is a cheese
native to the island of
Cyprus, and its name is
protected by Designation
of Origin status. When
purchasing the cheese,
look for authentic halloumi
produced on the island.

Using a knife, carefully remove the outer layer of zest from the lemons, leaving behind the bitter white pith. Cut the zest into thin strips.

Place the sugar in a saucepan with 200 ml (7 fl oz) of water and stir regularly over medium heat. When the liquid becomes syrupy, add the lemon zest strips and salt. Simmer for 7 minutes, then turn off the heat and leave to steep for 15 minutes.

In a frying pan, heat the olive oil and honey over high heat. Carefully place the halloumi slices in the hot oil and cook them for 3 minutes on each side, until golden brown.

Serve immediately, scattered with the candied lemon zest, and drizzled with any pan juices from the halloumi.

Note: *Halloumi should be served piping hot. When it cools, it becomes rubbery and less enjoyable.*

TARAMASALATA

SERVES 6

100 g (3½ oz) smoked cod roe,
  with membrane
50 g (1¾ oz) white bread
100 ml (3½ fl oz) milk
100 ml (3½ fl oz) grapeseed oil
zest of 1 lime
50 g (1¾ oz) creme fraiche
olive oil, for drizzling
dill sprigs, to serve (optional)
finely diced red onion, to serve
  (optional)
Sharwarma bread (page 150) or
  Rustic bread (page 153), to serve
  (optional)

Place the smoked cod roe in a bowl of cold water, cover and soak in the fridge for at least 2 hours, to remove the excess salt.

In another bowl, soak the bread in the milk for 30 minutes.

Using a slotted spoon, transfer the cod roe to a plate, then carefully peel away and discard the thin membrane surrounding it.

Remove the bread from the milk and squeeze it in-between your hands to remove as much liquid as possible.

Place the roe and bread in a blender and slowly pulse to combine. Once the mixture is smooth, add the grapeseed oil in a thin stream until emulsified.

Add the lime zest and creme fraiche and blend lightly.

Serve the taramasalata in a small bowl, drizzled with olive oil. It is delicious with sharwarma bread or rustic bread. Finish with dill or serve with some diced red onion on the side, if desired.

MARINATED MACKEREL
WITH HORSERADISH SAUCE

SERVES 6

6 mackerel fillets
200 g (7 oz) coarse salt
500 g (1 lb 2 oz) baby potatoes,
   unpeeled
3 thyme sprigs
3 bay leaves
2 garlic cloves, crushed
1 teaspoon salt
dill sprigs, to garnish

Marinade

250 ml (1 cup) apple cider vinegar
250 g (9 oz) granulated sugar
50 ml (1¾ fl oz) olive oil
1 garlic clove
3 bay leaves
4 cloves
2 teaspoons black peppercorns
2 teaspoons mustard seeds
1 teaspoon coriander seeds

Horseradish sauce

2 tablespoons olive oil
2 white onions, diced
250 g (1 cup) ricotta
2 bunches of dill
200 ml (7 fl oz) grapeseed oil
1 teaspoon grated horseradish

Place the mackerel fillets on a tray. Coat the fish with the coarse salt and rub it into the flesh. Transfer to the fridge to rest for 30 minutes.

Meanwhile, combine all the marinade ingredients in a saucepan. Bring to the boil, then transfer to a heatproof dish and leave to cool for 10 minutes.

Wipe the salt off the mackerel fillets. Submerge the fillets in the cooled marinade, then cover and refrigerate for 30 minutes. Just before serving, remove the thin, transparent film from the skin of the mackerel by loosening it with the tip of a knife, then pulling it off with your fingertips.

Fill a saucepan with 1.5 litres (6 cups) of cold water. Add the potatoes, thyme sprigs, bay leaves, garlic and salt. Bring to the boil, then let boil for 15–25 minutes, until the potatoes are soft and cooked through when pierced with a fork or the tip of a knife. Drain and set aside.

To make the horseradish sauce, place the olive oil and onion in a frying pan and simmer over low heat for about 10 minutes. Leave to cool slightly, then transfer the mixture to a blender. Add the ricotta and dill and pulse until smooth. Slowly incorporate the grapeseed oil until smooth. Add the horseradish and season to taste with salt and pepper.

To serve, place some horseradish sauce on a plate. Thinly slice the potatoes and place them on top, then drizzle with a little of the mackerel marinade. Top with the mackerel fillets and garnish with dill sprigs.

Note: *This dish can also be served as a main course served with mustard seed pickles (page 136), sliced red onion and a few kalamata olives, as shown in the photo.*

POLENTA CHIPS
WITH SPICY CRANBERRY SAUCE

SERVES 6

20 g (¾ oz) unsalted butter

1 tablespoon fine salt

250 g (2 cups) polenta

3 eggs

cornflour (corn starch), for coating

100 ml (3½ fl oz) sunflower oil

chopped parsley, to serve (optional)

charred green chillies, to serve
  (optional)

Spicy cranberry sauce

80 g (2¾ oz) granulated sugar

½ teaspoon salt

zest and juice of 1 orange

300 g (10½ oz) fresh cranberries
  (see Note)

1 small green chilli, seeded and
  finely chopped

Add 1.2 litres (41 fl oz) of water to a medium saucepan. Add the butter and salt. Bring to the boil, then reduce to a simmer. Gradually add the polenta, stirring vigorously with a wooden spoon until no lumps remain. Simmer for 10 minutes, stirring constantly.

Pour the polenta into a 30 cm × 24 cm (12 in × 9½ in) baking dish. Cover with plastic wrap and refrigerate for 30–45 minutes, or until cooled.

Meanwhile, make the spicy cranberry sauce. Place the sugar, salt, orange zest and juice in a saucepan. Add 50 ml (1¾ fl oz) of water and bring to the boil, then simmer over low heat until the sugar dissolves. Add the cranberries and simmer for 15 minutes, stirring occasionally. Remove from the heat, add the chilli and leave to cool, then pour into a blender and pulse to a chunky sauce consistency.

When ready to serve, cut the cooled polenta into eighteen sticks, each weighing about 60 g (2 oz). Beat the eggs in a bowl, and fill a small bowl with cornflour. Gently roll the polenta sticks in the egg, then in the cornflour to coat.

In a deep-sided frying pan, heat the sunflower oil to 180°C (350°F), or until a cube of bread dropped in the oil browns in 15 seconds. Working in batches, fry the coated polenta sticks for 2 minutes on each side, or until golden. Remove with a slotted spoon, drain on paper towel and season lightly with salt.

Serve immediately with the spicy cranberry sauce. If desired, sprinkle the polenta chips with parsley and serve with charred green chillies on the side.

Note: *If you're unable to source fresh cranberries, frozen cranberries that have been thawed will work as well.*

TAVENÝ
MORAVSKÝ
BOCHNÍK

SPOTREBUJTE DO 28 DNÍ OD DÁTUMU VÝROBY

Favorit

mer energia 1330kJ/100g
suš. 48 %   t.v.s 60 %
hmotnosť 227 g
ON 571301

Kčs
8,10

DISHES TO SHARE

WHEN DEVELOPING THE RECIPES
FOR THIS CHAPTER, I ASKED MYSELF WHAT
WOULD MAKE MY GUESTS HAPPIEST, AND
HOW I COULD BEST SATISFY THEM.

In other words, I did what most Balkan hosts do when
they learn they have to plan a large meal for guests:
pull out all the stops! Our go-to Balkan dishes are
generally very hearty, very tasty and very rich. They
echo our desire to live well – to pay homage to life, so
to speak – but also to thank nature for everything it
gives us every day.

BEEF KOFTAS
IN SPICY TOMATO SAUCE

SERVES 6

1 litre (4 cups) grapeseed oil
dill sprigs, to garnish

Spicy tomato sauce

100 ml (3½ fl oz) sunflower oil
400 g (14 oz) tinned finely
  chopped tomatoes
400 g (14 oz) tomato paste
  (concentrated puree)
100 ml (3½ fl oz) white wine
5 thyme sprigs
2 bay leaves
1 bunch of lovage
3 garlic cloves, crushed
130 g (4½ oz) granulated sugar
1 teaspoon Espelette chilli powder
  or chilli powder
1 teaspoon fine salt
1 teaspoon ground black pepper

Kofta

100 ml (3½ fl oz) sunflower oil
500 g (1 lb 2 oz) carrots, peeled
  and grated
2 large potatoes, peeled and grated
1.5 kg (3 lb 5 oz) minced (ground)
  beef, high in fat
3 eggs
3 onions, grated
4 garlic cloves, minced
2 bunches of dill, finely chopped
1 bunch of parsley, finely chopped
50 g (1¾ oz) fine dried breadcrumbs
1 teaspoon smoked paprika

To make the spicy tomato sauce, combine the sunflower oil, chopped tomatoes, tomato paste and wine in a large saucepan with 150 ml (5 fl oz) of water. Bring to a simmer over low heat, then leave to reduce for 20 minutes. Tie the thyme sprigs, bay leaves and lovage together to make a bouquet garni. Add it to the sauce, along with the remaining sauce ingredients. Simmer for another 30 minutes over low heat.

While the sauce is simmering, make the kofta. Heat the sunflower oil in a frying pan over medium heat and saute the carrot and potato for about 4 minutes, until tender. Remove from the heat and allow to cool.

Place the beef in a large bowl with the remaining kofta ingredients. Add the cooled sauteed vegetables. Season with salt and pepper and mix by hand for at least 10 minutes, until smooth and fluffy.

Cover the kofta mixture with plastic wrap and rest in the fridge for 30 minutes.

Using your hands, shape the kofta mixture into 18 round meatballs, weighing 90 g (3 oz) each.

In a saucepan with sides deep enough to avoid risk of splashing or boiling over, heat the grapeseed oil to 180°C (350°F), or until a cube of bread dropped in the oil browns in 15 seconds. Add the meatballs one by one and fry for 5 minutes, until their crust turns very dark. Remove with a slotted spoon and drain on paper towel.

Remove the pan of simmering sauce from the heat. Discard the bouquet garni and season to taste with salt and pepper. Using a hand-held stick blender, pulse the sauce until smooth.

Add the cooked kofta to the sauce, then bring back to a simmer over low heat. Simmer for another 15 minutes to develop the flavours.

Serve garnished with dill. This dish is delicious served with well-buttered mashed potatoes or polenta (page 101).

Note: *If you have any left-over kofta, they are delicious served cold the next day – in a sandwich, for example.*

PORK SARMA

SERVES 6

3.5 kg (7 lb 12 oz) Fermented cabbage
  (page 132), or 3 green cabbages
500 g (1 lb 2 oz) tinned finely
  chopped tomatoes
100 g (3½ oz) smoked bacon,
  thinly sliced
2 thyme sprigs
6 bay leaves

Filling

2 tablespoons sunflower oil
350 g (12½ oz) onions, diced
150 g (¾ cup) short-grain white rice
100 g (3½ oz) tomato paste
  (concentrated puree)
1 kg (2 lb 3 oz) minced (ground) pork,
  30% fat (pork belly, not sausage
  meat)
100 g (3½ oz) carrots, finely grated
2 teaspoons salt
1½ teaspoons sweet paprika
¾ teapoon smoked paprika
¾ teaspoon ground black pepper
¾ teaspoon dried thyme
pinch of Espelette chilli powder
  or chilli powder
75 ml (2½ fl oz) white wine

To make the filling, heat the sunflower oil in a frying pan over medium–low heat and gently cook the onion for a few minutes, until soft and transparent. Add the rice and stir constantly for 2–3 minutes, until the rice is translucent. Stir in the tomato paste and mix until smooth. Remove from the heat.

Place the pork in a large bowl with the remaining filling ingredients. Add the rice mixture and mix vigorously for about 10 minutes to combine. Cover with plastic wrap and refrigerate for 1–3 hours to allow all the flavours to blend.

If you are using fermented cabbage, separate the leaves, keeping the soft ones without holes and setting aside any damaged leaves. Using a sharp knife, make a cut at the base of the undamaged leaves and remove the tough parts at the bottom. Finely chop the tough parts and the damaged leaves and set aside to line the baking dish.

If you are using green cabbage, bring a large saucepan of water to the boil with a good pinch of coarse salt. Immerse one whole cabbage in the water. After 3–4 minutes, the first few leaves will peel off and you can then cut them away easily. Continue cooking and keep removing the leaves in this way until you reach the core. Place the leaves in a large bowl of iced water to stop the cooking process, then drain and dry them. Repeat with the other cabbages. The leaves are now ready to be stuffed. Finely chop a few leaves and set them aside to line the baking dish.

Preheat the oven to 170°C (340°F). Line the bottom of a large baking dish with half the finely chopped cabbage, to protect the rolls during cooking.

Place a cabbage leaf on your work surface, stem end nearest you. Place a tablespoonful of the filling – about 50 g (1¾ oz) – at the bottom of the leaf. Bring both sides of the leaf over the filling and roll it up tightly from the bottom to the tip. Repeat to make more rolls, until you've used up all the filling.

Arrange the rolls in the baking dish in tight rows, overlapping them if necessary. Cover the rolls with the remaining chopped cabbage.

Using a spatula, evenly spread the tomatoes over the rolls, then top with the bacon slices, thyme sprigs and bay leaves. Pour in enough water to cover the rolls, cover with foil and bake for 1 hour.

Remove the dish from the oven and carefully lift away the foil. Pour in water to cover the rolls again. Cover the dish with the foil and continue baking for another 2½ hours, until the cabbage is tender, the filling is firm and most of the liquid has reduced.

These rolls are lovely with creme fraiche and polenta chips (page 53).

DISHES TO SHARE

59

LAMB SHOULDER SHAWARMA
WITH POTATO CHIPS

SERVES 6

1.5 kg (3 lb 5 oz) boneless lamb
  shoulder (or leg)
2 teaspoons fine salt
3 tablespoons ground cumin
2 teaspoons Espelette chilli powder
  or chilli powder
5 garlic cloves, crushed
300 ml (10 fl oz) white wine
1 teaspoon timut peppercorns or
  Sichuan peppercorns
3 thyme sprigs
3 rosemary sprigs
6 Shawarma breads (page 150)
Pickled red onions (page 136)
3 large sweet and sour dill
  pickles (gherkins), sliced
  lengthways

Cabbage salad
½ white cabbage, finely shredded
2 tablespoons apple cider vinegar
1 tablespoon honey

Feta sauce
1 long hot green chilli, cut in half,
  seeded if desired
1 onion, diced
100 ml (3½ fl oz) olive oil
200 g (7 oz) feta, roughly chopped
200 g (7 oz) Greek-style yoghurt
200 ml (7 fl oz) creme fraiche

Potato chips
2 large potatoes, unpeeled
1 litre (4 cups) sunflower oil

Rub the lamb shoulder with the salt, place it in a freezer bag and refrigerate for 2 hours.

Rub the cumin and chilli powder all over the lamb, then nestle the garlic cloves in any cracks. Roll the lamb into a log and tie it up firmly using butcher's twine, to create a more uniform shape for even cooking and to keep the meat juicy. Place the lamb back in the freezer bag, add the wine and peppercorns and seal tightly. Marinate in the fridge overnight.

The next day, prepare the cabbage salad. Place the cabbage in a bowl and rub with sea salt. Cover and refrigerate for 3 hours, to let the cabbage release its water. Squeeze the cabbage vigorously to remove the excess moisture and place in a clean bowl. Mix the vinegar and honey and drizzle it over the cabbage. Set aside for serving.

Preheat the oven to 180°C (350°F).

Remove the lamb from the freezer bag, reserving the marinade, and place in a roasting tin. Add the thyme and rosemary sprigs, then pour the reserved marinade over. Cover with foil and bake for 45 minutes.

Reduce the oven to 150°C (300°F) and bake for another 45 minutes, occasionally basting the meat with its own juices.

Remove the foil and leave the lamb in the oven to brown for another 30 minutes.

Remove the lamb from the oven and let it rest in the dish for about 10 minutes. When cool enough to handle, shred the meat with two forks and let it rest in its own juices.

While the lamb is roasting, make the feta sauce. Crush the green chilli in a mortar to make a paste. Heat a drizzle of olive oil in a frying pan over medium heat and saute the onion for a few minutes, until soft. Transfer the onion to a blender and add the olive oil, feta, yoghurt and creme fraiche. Pulse at low speed until combined, then gradually add the green chilli paste, tasting after each addition, until you reach your desired level of spiciness. Season with salt if needed.

Just before serving, prepare the potato chips. Finely slice the potatoes into rounds, using a vegetable peeler. Place the slices in a deep bowl and wash them thoroughly. In a saucepan with sides deep enough to avoid splashing or boiling over, heat the sunflower oil to 180°C (350°F), or until a cube of bread dropped in the oil browns in 15 seconds. Add the potato slices and cook for 2–4 minutes, until nicely browned and crisp. Remove with a slotted spoon, drain on paper towel and season with salt.

To serve, top each shawarma bread with the shredded lamb, cabbage salad, pickled red onion and pickle slices. Drizzle the feta sauce over, then roll the bread up firmly and wrap with foil to secure the filling. Serve immediately, with the potato chips.

TRAVELLER'S SANDWICH

SERVES 6

1 good-quality loaf of unsliced bread
(preferably milk bread)

Crumbed chicken

1.2 kg (2 lb 10 oz) boneless, skinless
chicken breasts

750 ml (3 cups) buttermilk

2 garlic cloves, finely chopped

2 shallots, finely chopped

2 tablespoons sweet paprika

2 tablespoons fine salt

2 tablespoons ground black pepper

2 eggs

400 g (14 oz) panko crumbs or dried
breadcrumbs

sunflower oil or peanut oil, for
deep-frying

White cabbage slaw

1 kg (2 lb 3 oz) white cabbage, finely
shredded

1 heaped tablespoon salt

60 ml (¼ cup) sunflower oil

juice of ½ lemon

2 tablespoons apple cider vinegar

½ tablespoon honey

Egg sauce

6 eggs, at room temperature

1 bunch of parsley, finely chopped

1 bunch of chives, finely chopped

2 pickled or raw red onions, finely
diced

2 large dill pickles (gherkins,
preferably malossol), finely diced

juice of 1 lemon

3 tablespoons Mayonnaise (page 25)

> I have such fond childhood memories of this sandwich. When we took a train trip, my mother would often make two or three and wrap them in foil for us to enjoy along the way.

To prepare the crumbed chicken, start by placing the chicken breasts on a chopping board and pound them with a meat tenderiser or rolling pin until flat. In a bowl, mix together the buttermilk, garlic, shallot, paprika, salt and pepper, then add the chicken, ensuring it is coated all over. Cover with plastic wrap, then marinate in the fridge for at least 2 hours, or overnight for the best result.

Meanwhile, make the white cabbage slaw. Place the cabbage in a large bowl, sprinkle all over with the salt and knead with both hands to thoroughly rub the salt in, which will help soften the cabbage. Cover with plastic wrap and refrigerate for at least 2 hours.

Rinse the cabbage thoroughly and place in a large bowl. Whisk together the sunflower oil, lemon juice, vinegar and honey, pour the dressing over the cabbage and mix well.

To make the egg sauce, bring a large saucepan of water to the boil. Gently lower the eggs into the boiling water and let them simmer for 9 minutes. Remove with a slotted spoon and plunge them into cold water to stop the cooking process. Peel the eggs and crumble them into a bowl. Add the remaining ingredients and gently mix together. Season to taste with salt and pepper.

When you're ready to crumb the chicken, remove the marinated chicken breasts from the fridge and let them come back to room temperature.

Beat the eggs in a bowl, and put the panko crumbs in another bowl. Working with one piece at a time, roll the chicken in the egg, then in the panko crumbs.

Pour a generous amount of sunflower oil into a deep-sided frying pan or saucepan. Heat the oil to 180°C (350°F), or until a cube of bread dropped in the oil browns in 15 seconds. Add the chicken breasts and cook until the crust takes on a beautiful caramel colour. Remove using tongs and drain on paper towel.

Cut 12 generous slices of bread, each about 3 cm (1¼ in) thick. Spread half the slices with the egg sauce, then add a little slaw, a crumbed chicken breast and more egg sauce. Top with the remaining bread slices, then cut each sandwich in half and serve.

PASTITSIO

SERVES 6

500 g (1 lb 2 oz) bucatini or long
  macaroni
40 g (1½ oz) cascaval or emmental
  cheese, grated

Meat sauce

20 g (¾ oz) unsalted butter
60 ml (¼ cup) olive oil
200 g (7 oz) red onions, sliced
2 garlic cloves, sliced
500 g (1 lb 2 oz) minced (ground) beef
200 g (7 oz) minced (ground) pork
20 ml (¾ fl oz) red wine vinegar
200 ml (7 fl oz) chicken stock
800 g (1 lb 12 oz) tinned finely
  chopped tomatoes
2 cinnamon sticks
20 g (¾ oz) granulated sugar

Bechamel sauce

150 g (5½ oz) unsalted butter
150 g (1 cup) plain (all-purpose) flour
800 ml (27 fl oz) milk
3 egg yolks, beaten
pinch of nutmeg

Start by making the meat sauce. Heat the butter and half the olive oil in a frying pan over medium heat and saute the onion and garlic for a few minutes, until soft and translucent. Reduce the heat to very low and cook for about 20 minutes, until the onion is carmelised. Add the beef, pork and remaining olive oil, then leave for a few minutes, stirring occasionally. When the meat is browned and sticks to the pan slightly, stir in the vinegar to deglaze the pan. Add the stock, tomatoes, cinnamon sticks and half the sugar. Bring to the boil, then simmer over low heat for at least 50 minutes, until the sauce has reduced. Remove the cinnamon sticks, stir in the remaining sugar, then season to taste with salt and pepper. Set aside and keep warm.

Preheat the oven to 180°C (350°F). Butter or grease a 40 cm × 28 cm (16 in × 11 in) baking dish.

Fill a large saucepan with water, add a good pinch of salt and bring to the boil. Add the bucatini and cook for half the time indicated on the packet instructions. Drain, then arrange the bucatini lengthways in the baking dish. Spread the meat sauce over the pasta.

To make the bechamel sauce, melt the butter in a saucepan over low heat. Add the flour and cook for a few minutes, stirring frequently, until you have a smooth roux that is beginning to brown. Meanwhile, in a separate saucepan, heat the milk over low heat. Add the heated milk to the roux mixture, whisking continuously until smooth. Add the beaten egg yolks in three batches, whisking vigorously. Season to taste with nutmeg and salt.

Pour the bechamel sauce over the pasta dish and sprinkle with the grated cheese.

Bake for 45 minutes, or until the cheese is melted and deeply golden. Serve hot.

STUFFED PEPPERS

SERVES 6

12 long, sweet, fleshy red peppers, such as kapia
2 thyme sprigs
2 bay leaves

Filling

100 g (3½ oz) stale bread
2 tablespoons olive oil
1 white onion, diced
100 g (½ cup) white rice
70 g (2½ oz) tomato paste (concentrated puree)
500 g (1 lb 2 oz) high-fat minced (ground) beef
1 egg
2 garlic cloves, finely grated
1 bunch of parsley, finely chopped
1 bunch of dill, finely chopped
2 teaspoons herbes de Provence
2 teaspoons sweet paprika
1 teaspoon Espelette chilli powder or chilli powder

Tomato sauce

2 tablespoons olive oil
1 bunch of spring onions (scallions), finely chopped
100 ml (3½ fl oz) white wine
1 litre (4 cups) tomato puree
1 teaspoon brown sugar
2 celery stalks, finely chopped

To make the filling, put the stale bread in a bowl. Fill with water, cover and leave to soak in the fridge for 10–15 minutes, until softened.

Meanwhile, heat the olive oil in a frying pan and saute the onion over medium heat for a few minutes, until soft and translucent. Add the rice and 60 ml (¼ cup) of water and cook for another few minutes, until the rice is translucent. Stir in the tomato paste and remove from the heat.

Place the beef in a bowl. Drain the bread through a colander, removing as much moisture as possible, then add to the beef with the remaining filling ingredients. Add the rice mixture, season with fine salt and pepper and mix until combined.

Use a sharp knife to cut a thick stem cap off the top of each pepper, to use as 'lids' to seal the peppers during cooking. Set the stem tops aside. Remove the seeds from inside the peppers, then, using a knife, carefully remove as much of the white membrane as possible. This is a delicate process and can take some time, as the peppers are long and thin.

Place the filling mixture in a piping bag and gently fill the peppers with the stuffing; do not overstuff, or they will split while frying.

Preheat the oven to 170°C (340°F).

In a large, lightly oiled frying pan fry the peppers for 3–4 minutes per side, until the skins are browned.

Remove the grilled peppers from the pan. Secure the stems on top using toothpicks.

To make the tomato sauce, heat the olive oil in a frying pan over medium heat and quickly saute the spring onion, until translucent and softened. Stir in the wine to deglaze the pan, then add the tomato puree, sugar, celery and 100 ml (3½ fl oz) of water. Season to taste with salt and pepper.

Pour the tomato sauce into a deep baking dish. Arrange the stuffed peppers lengthways in the dish, side by side. Scatter the thyme sprigs and bay leaves on top, then cover with foil.

Bake for 45 minutes, then remove the foil and bake for another 15 minutes until the pepper skins are blistered and slightly browned, and the flesh is tender.

POTATO MOUSSAKA

IBRIK

SERVES 6

1 kg (2 lb 3 oz) potatoes, unpeeled
1 tablespoon coarse salt
2 garlic cloves
1 thyme sprig
1 bay leaf
200 g (7 oz) dried breadcrumbs
Rustic bread (page 153), to serve
  (optional)

Beef filling

2 tablespoons olive oil
4 white onions, diced
pinch of salt
100 g (3½ oz) unsalted butter
800 g (1 lb 12 oz) minced (ground)
  beef
1 tablespoon tomato paste
  (concentrated puree)
8 garlic cloves, minced
2 teaspoons chilli powder
2 teaspoons smoked paprika
600 g (1 lb 5 oz) tinned finely
  chopped tomatoes
4 bay leaves
4 thyme sprigs
1 tablespoon granulated sugar

Bechamel sauce

150 g (5½ oz) unsalted butter
150 g (1 cup) plain (all-purpose) flour
800 ml (27 fl oz) milk
3 egg yolks
pinch of nutmeg

To make the beef filling, heat the olive oil in a frying pan over high heat and saute the onion with the salt for a few minutes, until soft and translucent. Add the butter, then the beef, and saute for another few minutes, until the meat releases some water. Add the tomato paste and simmer for a few more minutes. Stir in the garlic, chilli powder and paprika, then set aside.

Place the chopped tomatoes, bay leaves and thyme sprigs in a large saucepan and infuse over medium heat for 5 minutes. Stir in the beef mixture, then cook for a further 15 minutes, stirring regularly. Season to taste with salt, pepper and the sugar, if the sauce is too tangy. Remove from the heat and set aside.

While the beef filling is simmering, place the potatoes in a large saucepan of cold water with the salt, garlic, thyme sprig and bay leaf. Bring to the boil, then cook for 20 minutes, until the potatoes are almost cooked through, but the core is still firm. Drain the potatoes, then rinse under cold water. Peel the skins off, then thinly slice the potatoes and set aside.

Preheat the oven to 170°C (340°F).

In a large gratin dish or individual dishes, arrange a layer of the beef filling, then add a layer of potato slices. Add another beef layer, then top with more potato slices.

To make the bechamel sauce, melt the butter in a saucepan over low heat. Add the flour and cook for a few minutes, stirring frequently, until you have a smooth roux that is beginning to brown. Meanwhile, in a separate saucepan, heat the milk over low heat. Add the heated milk to the roux mixture, whisking continuously until smooth. Add the beaten egg yolks in three batches, whisking vigorously. Season to taste with nutmeg and salt.

Pour the bechamel sauce over the moussaka and sprinkle with the breadcrumbs.

Bake for 25 minutes, until the crumb topping is golden brown and crispy.

If desired, serve with rustic bread on the side.

CHICKEN GOULASH

SERVES 6

1.2 kg (2 lb 10 oz) boneless, skinless
  chicken breasts, diced
60 ml (¼ cup) sunflower oil
1 teaspoon black peppercorns
1½ teaspoons sweet paprika
¾ teaspoon smoked paprika
220 g (8 oz) tomato paste
  (concentrated puree)
450 g (1 lb) onions, diced
300 g (10½ oz) carrots, diced
175 g (6 oz) celeriac, diced
100 g (3½ oz) parsnips, diced
85 g (3 oz) tinned finely
  chopped tomatoes
2 bay leaves
1 thyme sprig
5 garlic cloves, finely chopped
3½ teaspoons salt
1 teaspoon ground turmeric
1 teaspoon coriander seeds
finely chopped parsley, to garnish

Place the chicken in a bowl with half the sunflower oil and a pinch of salt. Mix well and leave to marinate for 5 minutes.

In a non-stick frying pan over high heat, fry the chicken cubes for 3–4 minutes per side until golden brown, then transfer to a plate.

Pour the remaining 30 ml (1 fl oz) of oil into a saucepan over medium heat and fry the peppercorns, sweet and smoked paprika and tomato paste for 1 minute. Stir in the onion and sweat for a few minutes, until softened.

Add the carrot, celeriac, parsnip, chopped tomatoes, bay leaves and thyme sprig. Cover with the lid and bring the mixture to the boil, then add the chicken, along with the garlic, salt, turmeric and coriander. Season with pepper and stir in 300 ml (10 fl oz) of water.

Put the lid back on, reduce the heat and simmer gently for 45 minutes, until the chicken is tender.

Serve sprinkled with parsley. This goulash is delicious served with grilled halloumi (page 46) or beetroot salad (page 37) on the side.

Note: *The quality of the paprika is the key to a good goulash. If possible, use Hungarian paprika, along with good-quality tomato paste and tomatoes.*

DISHES TO SHARE

BEEF TONGUE
WITH KALAMATA OLIVES

SERVES 6

3 carrots, roughly chopped
3 celery stalks, roughly chopped
1 white onion, quartered
8 garlic cloves
1.7 kg (3 lb 12 oz) beef tongue
½ bunch of thyme
½ bunch of rosemary
3 cloves
2 star anise
2 cardamom pods
1 cinnamon stick
1 tablespoon coarse salt

Tomato sauce with olives
2 tablespoons olive oil
1.2 kg (2 lb 10 oz) tinned finely
   chopped tomatoes
2 onions, sliced
2 garlic cloves, sliced
3 celery stalks, diced
4 bay leaves
200 g (7 oz) kalamata olives, pitted
1 teaspoon granulated sugar

Put the carrot, celery, onion and garlic in a large saucepan. Place the beef tongue on top. Add the herbs and spices, then fill with water. Bring to the boil, skimming off any impurities that rise to the surface with a slotted spoon.

Reduce the heat and simmer gently for 2 hours. Add the salt and 2.5 litres (10 cups) of water, then simmer for another 2 hours, until the tongue is tender.

Remove the tongue from the broth. When cool enough to handle, peel off any remaining skin. Place the tongue on a plate, cover with plastic wrap and refrigerate overnight.

The next day, make the tomato sauce. Heat the olive oil in a saucepan over high heat and fry the tomato, onion and garlic for 3 minutes. Add the celery, bay leaves, olives and sugar. Mix well, then reduce the heat and simmer for 45 minutes.

Slice the tongue into 5 cm × 2 cm (2 in × ¾ in) rectangles. Add them to the sauce and simmer over low heat for another 15 minutes, until heated through.

Season to taste with salt and pepper, then serve.

Note: *You can save the broth and vegetables (from poaching the beef tongue) to make soup or cook pasta in. You can also freeze the broth for later use.*

PORK SHANK HOTPOT WITH CREAMY BURGHUL

SERVES 6

1 pomegranate, halved
1 kg (2 lb 3 oz) pork shank
grapeseed oil, for pan-frying
4 carrots, finely chopped
2 shallots, finely chopped
3 garlic cloves, finely chopped
1 fennel bulb, finely chopped
½ bunch of sage
3 bay leaves
1¾ teapspoons salt
1 teaspoon black peppercorns
400 ml (13½ fl oz) chicken stock

Sweet smoky cabbage

500 g (1 lb 2 oz) white cabbage,
  finely shredded
20 g (¾ oz) salt
1 tablespoon grapeseed oil
50 g (1¾ oz) smoked bacon
1 tablespoon honey

Caramelised onions

60 g (2 oz) granulated sugar
½ star anise
1 teaspoon coriander seeds
3 red onions, unpeeled

Creamy burghul

600 g (1 lb 5 oz) Greek-style yoghurt
120 g (4½ oz) burghul
1 teaspoon salt
100 ml (3½ fl oz) cream (35% fat)

To prepare the sweet smoky cabbage, put the cabbage in a bowl, add the salt and mix well. Cover with plastic wrap, then refrigerate for 3 hours, to help release the excess water.

Rinse the cabbage in cold water, then place it in a clean thin tea towel and squeeze until the water is gone. Heat the grapeseed oil in a frying pan (preferably cast iron) over high heat and saute the cabbage for about 15 minutes, until softened. Reduce the heat to medium, add the bacon and honey, then saute for another 10 minutes, until the bacon is cooked. Remove from the heat and set aside.

Preheat the oven to 180°C (350°F).

Extract the seeds from the pomegranate by lightly tapping the pomegranate skin with a spatula. Remove any remaining white membrane from the seeds as it is bitter. Set the seeds aside.

Season the pork shank with salt. Heat a generous drizzle of oil in a flameproof casserole dish over high heat. Add the shank and cook for about 5 minutes per side, or until golden brown all over. Add the carrot, shallot and garlic and cook for 5–8 minutes to brown the vegetables and release their juices. Add half the pomegranate seeds, fennel, sage, bay leaves, salt and peppercorns. Pour in the stock and bring back to the boil. Cover the dish, place in the oven and bake for 1½ hours, or until the meat is very tender.

While the shank is baking in the oven, prepare the caramelised onions. In a saucepan, combine the sugar, star anise, coriander seeds and 1 teaspoon of water. Let the mixture dissolve over low heat for 1 minute to form a syrup, then pour this syrup into a baking dish. Cut the red onions in half, leaving the skin on, and place them in the syrup, cut side down. Cover the dish with foil and bake at 180°C (350°F) for 40 minutes, until the onions are soft. Remove them from the oven and leave to cool for a few minutes, then peel off the skin and set aside on a plate at room temperature.

Near serving time, prepare the creamy burghul. Place the yogurt, burghul and salt in a saucepan and whisk together over medium heat, then cook for 15–20 minutes, stirring constantly. Stir in the cream and set aside for serving.

Once the shank is cooked, remove the casserole dish from the oven and add the sweet smoky cabbage and caramelised onions. Put the lid back on, to gently reheat the cabbage and onion until hot.

Serve with the creamy burghul sprinkled with the remaining pomegranate seeds.

HUMMUS WITH SPICED BEEF

IBRIK

SERVES 6

Hummus

360 g (1⅔ cups) dried chickpeas
  (garbanzo beans)
150 ml (5 fl oz) sunflower oil
juice of 1 lemon
3 garlic cloves
30 g (1 oz) tahini
1½ teaspoons ground cumin
1 teaspoon salt

Spiced beef

2 tablespoons olive oil
2 onions, diced
4 thyme sprigs
2 teaspoons ground cinnamon
1 teaspoon buknu masala (see Notes)
1.2 kg (2 lb 10 oz) minced (ground)
  beef
2 garlic cloves, chopped
1¼ teaspoons salt
½ teaspoon ground black pepper

To serve

Dill pickles (page 135)
Pickled red onions (page 136)
Espelette chilli powder or chilli
  powder, for sprinkling
olive oil, for drizzling
Pita bread (page 154; omit to keep
  recipe gluten free)

To make the hummus, place the dried chickpeas in a large bowl. Pour 1 litre (4 cups) of cold water over the chickpeas, cover with plastic wrap, then leave to soak overnight in the fridge.

The next day, drain the chickpeas, then place in a large saucepan with plenty of cold water. Bring to the boil, then reduce the heat and leave to simmer for 2 hours, until the chickpeas are tender.

Drain the chickpeas, reserving 150 ml (5 fl oz) of the cooking water. Transfer the cooked chickpeas to a blender or food processor. Add the sunflower oil, lemon juice, garlic, tahini, cumin and salt, then puree for 7–10 minutes. Gradually add small amounts of the reserved cooking water until you have a smooth paste. Set aside for serving.

To prepare the spiced beef, heat the olive oil in a frying pan over high heat. Add the onion and thyme and cook for 8–10 minutes until the onion is golden brown and softened, then add in the cinnamon and buknu masala and fry for another minute to bring out the flavours of the spices.

Reduce the heat to medium and add the beef, breaking it up with a wooden spoon. Once the meat is browned and almost cooked, stir in the garlic, salt and pepper. Leave to simmer over low heat for 20 minutes, or until the liquid has evaporated. Remove the thyme.

Transfer the hummus to a serving bowl, make a well in the centre and pile the spiced beef on top. Garnish with dill pickles and red onions, add a sprinkle of chilli powder and serve drizzled with a dash of olive oil. If desired, enjoy with pita bread.

Notes: *For an even smoother and creamier hummus, you can remove the skin of the cooked chickpeas before blending them by rubbing them between your hands with a clean towel. The skins will peel off easily.*

If you can't find buknu masala, you can replace with an equal measure of garam masala mixed with a pinch of ground cloves and nutmeg.

STUFFED SQUID

SERVES 6

6 whole squid, about 10–15 cm
  (4–6 in) long
60 ml (¼ cup) olive oil
1 tablespoon butter
3 yellow zucchini (courgettes),
  finely diced
3 green zucchini (courgettes),
  finely diced
4 garlic cloves, chopped
1 bunch of dill, chopped
20 kalamata olives, roughly chopped
½ teaspoon Espelette chilli powder
  or chilli powder
1¼ teaspoons ground black pepper
3 thyme sprigs
pinch of sweet paprika
chopped dill, to garnish
lemon zest, to garnish

Aioli

2 eggs, at room temperature
1 egg yolk
3 garlic cloves, finely grated
40 ml (1¼ fl oz) lemon juice
1 teaspoon dijon mustard
150 ml (5 fl oz) sunflower oil

To make the aioli, bring a saucepan of water to the boil. Gently lower the eggs into the boiling water and cook for 8 minutes. Remove with a slotted spoon and plunge them into a bowl of cold water to stop the cooking process. Peel the eggs and remove the yolks, reserving the whites for another purpose. Place the two yolks in a bowl with the raw egg yolk. Add the garlic, lemon juice and mustard. Using an immersion blender fitted with a whisk, blend until smooth. Slowly add the sunflower oil, whisking vigorously until the aioli has thickened like mayonnaise. Cover and refrigerate for serving.

Preheat the oven to 180°C (350°F). Line a baking tray with baking paper.

Rinse the squid in cold water. Holding the squid's body in one hand, pull the tentacles out with the other. Cut the tentacles just below the squid's beak and set them aside. Remove the transparent part of the squid's body by pulling it out. Using a knife (or by pulling on it with your fingers), scrape the surface to remove the brown skin. With your fingers, check that nothing remains inside the body. Set the squid aside.

Heat the olive oil in a frying pan over high heat. Add the butter, zucchini, garlic and half the dill and saute for 5–6 minutes, until the zucchini is tender. Remove from the heat, stir in the olives, chilli powder and pepper, then season with salt. Leave to cool, then transfer the mixture to a piping bag. Set aside the pan for frying the squid tentacles later on.

Stuff the squid bodies with the zucchini mixture, then briefly sear the squid in a lightly oiled frying pan over high heat.

Place the stuffed squid on the lined baking tray. Arrange the thyme sprigs on top, then bake for 8 minutes.

Meanwhile, roughly chop the squid tentacles. Place them in the pan you cooked the zucchini in. Add the remaining dill and a drizzle of olive oil and saute over high heat for 3–5 minutes, until browned and crisp on the edges. Season to taste with a pinch of sweet paprika and salt.

Serve immediately, alongside the stuffed squid and aioli, garnished with dill and lemon zest.

BAKED SEA BASS
WITH SPICY TAHINI SAUCE

SERVES 6

1.5 kg (3 lb 5 oz) small creamy
   yellow-fleshed potatoes, such as
   charlotte, peeled and sliced 5 mm
   (¼ in) thick
3 onions, sliced
200 ml (7 fl oz) white wine
40 g (1½ oz) pomegranate molasses
2.4 kg (5 lb 5 oz) whole sea bass,
   gutted
½ bunch of coriander (cilantro)
½ bunch of thyme
3 garlic cloves, minced
½ bunch of rosemary
50 ml (1¾ fl oz) olive oil

Spicy tahini sauce

175 ml (6 fl oz) cream
175 g (6 oz) tahini
120 ml (4 fl oz) milk
2 garlic cloves, minced
juice of ½ lemon
½ red chilli pepper, finely chopped
1 bunch of coriander (cilantro),
   finely chopped

Preheat the oven to 210°C (410°F).

Place the potato slices and onion in a baking dish. In a bowl, mix together the wine, pomegranate molasses and 200 ml (7 fl oz) of water and pour over the potatoes. Bake for 15 minutes, then remove from the oven.

Meanwhile, season the fish inside and out with salt and pepper. Place the coriander and thyme inside its belly. In a bowl, mix together the garlic, rosemary and olive oil and brush all over the fish, then place the fish on top of the baked potatoes. Bake for 20 minutes, then check if the fish is cooked – the flesh should be pearly. If not, cover the dish with foil and bake for an additional 15 minutes.

Just before serving, make the spicy tahini sauce. In a saucepan, combine the cream, tahini, milk, garlic, lemon juice and chilli over low heat. Simmer for 2 minutes, then remove from the heat and stir in the coriander. Season to taste with salt and pepper.

Serve the fish and potatoes with the spicy tahini sauce.

BAKED COD AND ORZO RISOTTO

SERVES 6

2 tablespoons olive oil, plus extra
  for drizzling
2 onions, diced
2 garlic cloves, finely grated
1 tablespoon sweet paprika
1 teaspoon ground cinnamon
1 teaspoon brown sugar
1 kg (2 lb 3 oz) juicy tomatoes,
  finely chopped
4 red bell peppers (capsicums),
  finely chopped
2 large leeks, finely chopped
1 tablespoon tomato paste
  (concentrated puree)
500 ml (2 cups) passata (pureed
  tomatoes)
1 bunch of oregano, leaves chopped
1 bunch of parsley, chopped
200 ml (7 fl oz) white wine
1.2 kg (2 lb 10 oz) skinless cod fillets
juice of 1 lemon
2 thyme sprigs
2 bay leaves
500 g (1 lb 2 oz) orzo or other
  small pasta
grilled or baked lemon slices, to serve
  (optional)

Orzo is a popular pasta in
the Balkans, and is often
used as a substitute for
rice. Add orzo to your
favourite soups to give
them a thicker texture.

Preheat the oven to 180°C (350°F).

Heat the olive oil in a large frying pan over medium–low heat and saute the onion for a few minutes, until soft and translucent. Add the garlic, paprika, cinnamon and sugar and briefly saute over medium heat.

Add the chopped tomatoes, bell pepper, leek, tomato paste, passata, oregano and half the chopped parsley. Mix until well combined, then stir in the wine. Season with salt and pepper and leave to reduce over medium heat for about 15 minutes. Remove from the heat.

Dry the fish fillets thoroughly, then season with salt and pepper. Place the fish in a baking dish and drizzle with the lemon juice. Pour the tomato mixture over the fish. Add the thyme sprigs, bay leaves and a generous drizzle of olive oil.

Bake for 15 minutes, then remove the dish from the oven, but leave the oven on.

While the fish is baking, add a good pinch of salt to a large saucepan of water and bring to the boil. Add the orzo and cook for three-quarters of the time indicated on the packet.

Drain the orzo and add it to the baking dish around the fish, making sure to submerge all the orzo in the sauce.

Return the dish to the oven and continue baking for 20–25 minutes until both the orzo and fish are cooked through and the orzo is soaked in the fish juices.

Serve sprinkled with the remaining parsley and, if desired, lemon slices.

PRAWNS WITH DILL
AND ONION PILAF

SERVES 6

6 unpeeled large prawns (shrimp),
  about 150 g (5½ oz) each, or
  12 small prawns
1–2 tablespoons sunflower oil
2 garlic cloves, finely grated
3 tablespoons pastis or ouzo
½ bunch of dill, finely chopped

Broth

3 bay leaves
2 thyme sprigs
2 teaspoons red baharat, Espelette
  chilli powder or chilli powder
2 garlic cloves, halved
1 teaspoon timut peppercorns or
  Sichuan peppercorns
500 ml (2 cups) white wine
1 litre (4 cups) cream

Dill and onion pilaf

1–2 tablespoons sunflower oil
2 red onions, diced
1 onion, diced
350 g (1¾ cups) basmati or
  jasmine rice
1½ bunches of dill, finely chopped

To prepare the broth, put the bay leaves and one thyme sprig in a saucepan, pour in 1 litre (4 cups) of water, season with salt and bring to the boil. Reduce to a simmer, add the whole prawns and cook for 10 minutes if using large prawns, or 5–6 minutes if using small prawns.

Remove the prawns with a slotted spoon, reserving the broth for the pilaf. Peel the prawns, placing the heads and peelings in a saucepan. Devein the prawns and set aside.

To the pan with the prawn heads and peelings, add the baharat, garlic cloves, peppercorns and remaining thyme sprig and saute over high heat for 6–7 minutes, until the prawn peelings turn pinkish orange. Add half the wine and stir to deglaze the pan. Add the remaining wine and simmer for 5 minutes, or until reduced by half. Stir in the cream, then reduce the heat to low and continue to cook for 8–10 minutes, until slightly thickened.

Remove the creamy broth from the heat and strain into another pan through a fine sieve. Press with a ladle to extract all the juices from the prawn peelings. Set the sauce aside, keeping it warm for serving.

To prepare the dill and onion pilaf, heat the sunflower oil in a saucepan and fry the onions over medium heat for a few minutes, until soft and translucent. Add the rice and stir constantly for a 2–3 minutes, until the grains are translucent. When the grains become translucent, use a ladle to gradually pour in the prawn cooking broth. Repeat, stirring and adding a ladleful of broth at a time, until the rice is cooked – it will take about 15 minutes. Remove from the heat, stir in the dill and season with salt to taste.

In a frying pan, heat the sunflower oil and garlic over high heat. Carefully place the prawns in the pan and saute for 1 minute. Deglaze the pan with the pastis, add the dill and cook for another 3 minutes, or until the prawns are nicely seared all over.

Pile the dill and onion pilaf into shallow serving bowls, top with the seared prawns, drizzle with the creamy sauce and serve.

Note: *If using frozen prawns, let them thaw before cooking.*

SEAFOOD BRODET

SERVES 6

200 g (7 oz) clams

200 g (7 oz) raw prawns (shrimp)

200 g (7 oz) skinless sea bass fillets

200 g (7 oz) skinless john dory fillets

200 g (7 oz) skinless tuna fillets

2 tablespoons olive oil

2 shallots, diced

3 garlic cloves, finely chopped

1 sweet red chilli, finely chopped

2 tablespoons white wine vinegar

1 teaspoon red baharat (see Note)

200 ml (7 fl oz) white wine

500 g (1 lb 2 oz) cherry tomatoes,
  cut in half

300 g (10½ oz) passata (pureed
  tomatoes)

1 teaspoon pink peppercorns

1 teaspoon timut peppercorns or
  Sichuan peppercorns

½ bunch of parsley, finely chopped

Soak the clams in cold salted water for 30 minutes, stirring regularly; the shells should open and release any sand. Rinse the clams thoroughly in cold water.

Bring a small saucepan of salted water to the boil and add the prawns. Cook for 1–2 minutes, until they are partially pink, then remove them using a slotted spoon. When cool enough to handle, peel the prawns.

Dry all the fish fillets with paper towel, then season with salt and pepper. Cut into bite-sized chunks.

Heat the olive oil in a large deep frying pan over medium heat. Add the shallot and fry for several minutes, until translucent. Add the garlic, chilli, vinegar and baharat and saute for 30 seconds.

Increase the heat to high, then add the fish, prawns and clams. Cook for 2–3 minutes, taking care not to break up the fish. Add the wine to deglaze the pan, then leave to simmer for a few minutes.

Add the cherry tomatoes, passata and peppercorns. Reduce the heat to low, cover and simmer for 1 hour, shaking the pan occasionally to loosen the ingredients and stop them sticking. (Avoid mixing with a spatula, to avoid breaking up the fish.) If any clams haven't opened after cooking, remove and discard.

Serve sprinkled with the chopped parsley.

Note: *If you can't find red baharat, you can replace with an equal measure of chilli flakes, ground paprika and coriander seeds mixed together.*

IBRIK

GRILLED TROUT AND
JERUSALEM ARTICHOKE MOUSSELINE

SERVES 6

6 trout, about 200–300 g
  (7–10½ oz) each, gutted
3 lemons, sliced
sunflower oil, for greasing

Mousseline

2 tablespoons plain (all-purpose) flour
zest and juice of 1 lemon
1 kg (2 lb 3 oz) Jerusalem artichokes,
  peeled and cut into equal-sized
  pieces
100 ml (3½ fl oz) cream (35% fat)
25 g (1 oz) unsalted butter

To serve

Mustard seed pickles (page 136)
Pickled red onions (page 136)
lemon slices
dill sprigs

To prepare the mousseline, mix the flour with the lemon zest and juice in a large bowl. Mix in about 1.5 litres (6 cups) of water, then add the Jerusalem artichokes, to prevent browning.

In a saucepan, bring 3 litres (3 quarts) of water to the boil. Remove the artichokes from the flour mixture and rinse. Add to the boiling water and cook for 20–25 minutes, until tender.

Meanwhile, preheat the oven to 170°C (340°F). Rinse the trout in cold water and pat dry with paper towel. Using scissors, trim the fins and tails. Season the insides of each trout with salt and pepper, then place the lemon slices inside each fish.

In an oiled chargrill pan over low heat, grill the trout for 3–4 minutes per side, until the skin is crisp and lightly browned.

Transfer the grilled trout to a baking dish and finish cooking in the oven for 8–10 minutes, or until the flesh is pearly. Remove the lemon slices from the fish.

Drain the artichokes and, while still warm, place in a food processor. Add the cream and butter and pulse the mixture until creamy. Season to taste with salt and pepper.

Serve the grilled trout with the mousseline on the side, finished with mustard seed pickles, pickled red onions, lemon slices and dill sprigs.

DISHES TO SHARE

ÇILBIR (FRIED EGGS WITH YOGHURT)

SERVES 6

3 fennel bulbs
90 ml (3 fl oz) olive oil
2 tablespoons honey
50 g (1¾ oz) hazelnuts
85 g (3 oz) unsalted butter
12 eggs
1 tablespoon sweet paprika
dill sprigs, to garnish
Rustic bread (page 153), to serve
    (optional; omit to keep
    recipe gluten free)

Garlic yoghurt sauce

1 kg (4 cups) Greek-style yoghurt
6 garlic cloves, finely grated
juice of 1 lemon
pinch of red baharat, Espelette chilli
    powder or chilli powder

✽ ⚘

Çilbir is usually made
with soft-boiled or
poached eggs, but here
we've offered a twist
with fried eggs.

To make the garlic yoghurt sauce, line a colander with muslin (cheesecloth) or a clean thin tea towel. Place the colander over a bowl, pour the yoghurt into it and cover. Let the yoghurt drain in the fridge overnight to remove the excess liquid.

The next day, preheat the oven to 170°C (340°F).

Cut the fennel bulbs into quarters, then remove the tough, stringy parts with a knife.

Pour the olive oil and honey into a frying pan and add the fennel and a pinch of salt. Over low heat, caramelise the fennel for about 10 minutes, until golden brown all over, turning often.

Transfer the fennel to a baking dish and drizzle with the pan juices. Cover the dish with foil, place in the oven and bake for 30 minutes. Remove the foil and bake for another 10 minutes, until the fennel is tender all the way through.

Meanwhile, place the hazelnuts on a baking tray and roast in the oven for 5 minutes. Remove from the oven and leave to cool, then roughly chop and set aside.

Place the strained yoghurt in a large bowl, add the remaining ingredients and mix until combined. Just before serving, spread the yoghurt sauce over six serving plates.

To cook the eggs, melt 1 tablespoon of butter in a frying pan over medium heat. Gently crack two eggs into the pan and leave to fry for 2–3 minutes. Slide the eggs onto one of the serving plates, then repeat with the remaining eggs.

In the same pan, vigorously stir the sweet paprika into the buttery cooking pan juices, taking care to avoid burning the paprika. Remove from the heat.

Arrange the roasted fennel on each plate, next to the eggs. Sprinkle with the chopped hazelnuts, drizzle with the paprika butter and garnish with dill sprigs. If desired, serve with rustic bread on the side.

MENEMEN AND MINT CREAM

SERVES 6

50 ml (1¾ fl oz) olive oil

10 kapia peppers, or other small sweet red peppers

3 onions, finely sliced

4 garlic cloves, finely grated

1 kg (2 lb 3 oz) tinned finely chopped tomatoes

150 g (5½ oz) cherry tomatoes

1 tablespoon ground cumin

1 teaspoon fine salt

1 teaspoon ground black pepper

1 teaspoon baharat, Espelette chilli powder or chilli powder

5 thyme sprigs

5 bay leaves

12 eggs

100 ml (3½ fl oz) milk

3 leeks, finely sliced

1 tablespoon butter

shredded mint, to garnish

Rustic bread (page 153), to serve (optional; omit to keep recipe gluten free)

Mint cream

½ bunch of mint, chopped

1 garlic clove, finely grated

250 ml (1 cup) cream (35% fat)

squeeze of lemon juice

pinch of fine salt

Heat a drizzle of the olive oil in a chargrill pan over high heat. Grill seven of the peppers, turning often, for 8–10 minutes, or until their skins are charred all over. Place them in a bowl, cover with plastic wrap, and set aside at room temperature for 30 minutes. Once cooled, peel off their skins, roughly chop the flesh and set aside.

Dice the remaining three peppers. Heat another drizzle of olive oil in a large frying pan over high heat, then fry the chopped pepper and onion for 5 minutes, stirring regularly.

Reduce the heat to medium, add the garlic and saute for 1 minute. Add the chopped tomatoes and grilled pepper, then reduce the heat and simmer for 10 minutes.

Stir in the cherry tomatoes, cumin, salt, pepper, baharat, thyme sprigs and bay leaves. Let the sauce reduce over low heat for 20 minutes, stirring occasionally. Remove the thyme and bay leaves, set aside and keep warm.

Place the mint cream ingredients in a food processor and blend until the cream is thick and fluffy.

When ready to serve, crack the eggs into a bowl and whisk vigorously. Add the milk, season with salt and pepper and whisk until combined.

Heat the remaning olive oil in a frying pan over medium heat and saute the leek for 3–5 minutes until translucent. Pour in the egg. When the bottom begins to cook, stir the eggs with a spatula, always pushing in the same direction, until the eggs are cooked but still creamy. Finish by mixing in the butter.

Serve the scrambled eggs in the tomato and pepper sauce, topped with the mint cream and garnished with shredded mint. Enjoy with rustic bread on the side, if desired.

BOUYOURDI (BAKED FETA DIP)

SERVES 6

600 g (1 lb 5 oz) feta
90 ml (3 fl oz) olive oil, plus extra
  for brushing
6 garlic cloves, crushed
2 onions, diced
6 kapia peppers, or other small sweet
  red peppers, sliced into strips
300 g (10½ oz) leeks, finely sliced
18 bay leaves
600 g (1 lb 5 oz) cherry tomatoes,
  halved
dried or fresh oregano, for sprinkling

We usually enjoy
bouyourdi in the summer
in village tavernas.

Preheat the oven to 180°C (350°F).

Slice the feta lengthways into 12 slices, weighing about 50 g (1¾ oz) each.

Grease six 10 cm (4 in) ramekins or ovenproof dishes with a little olive oil. Rub some of the garlic inside each one and place one slice of feta at the bottom of each.

Next, divide the garlic, onion, kapia pepper, leek, bay leaves and cherry tomatoes between the dishes.

Place a second slice of feta on top of each. Sprinkle with oregano and plenty of pepper, then drizzle 15 ml (½ fl oz) of olive oil over each.

Bake for 25 minutes, until the feta has softened and lightly carmelised.

Serve in the ramekins, straight from the oven.

Note: *If you don't have small ramekins, you can simply assemble and cook the dish in individual baking paper parcels. And don't be afraid to add a little more garlic – the dish will be even tastier!*

POLENTA STUFFED WITH CHEESE AND CREME FRAICHE

SERVES 6

1 teaspoon sea salt
25 g (1 oz) butter
300 g (10½ oz) polenta
250 g (9 oz) soft sheep's milk cheese,
  such as Brânză de Burduf
olive oil, for drizzling
800 g (1 lb 12 oz) creme fraiche
Pickled red onions (page 136), to serve
black and white sesame seeds,
  for sprinkling

❋ ⚜

This very rustic dish is
traditionally enjoyed
by shepherds. We've
glammed it a little, but the
taste remains the same.

Preheat the oven to 170°C (340°F). Line a baking tray with baking paper.

Pour 1.4 litres (47 fl oz) of water into a large saucepan, add the salt and butter and bring to the boil. Gradually pour in the polenta, stirring vigorously with a whisk until no lumps remain. Cook for 10 minutes over low heat, stirring frequently. Remove from the heat and leave to cool.

Grate the cheese and shape into small balls about 15 g (½ oz) each.

Wet your hands and spread about 2 tablespoons of the cooled polenta in the palm of your hand. Place a ball of cheese in the centre and wrap the polenta around the cheese, then shape into a smooth sphere. Repeat with the remaining polenta and cheese.

Arrange the polenta balls on the lined baking tray. Drizzle with a little olive oil, then bake for 10 minutes, until golden.

Serve the warm polenta balls on a bed of creme fraiche, garnished with pickled red onions and sesame seeds.

DISHES TO SHARE

THREE CHEESE PIDE

SERVES 6

3 leeks, cut into rounds 5 mm (¼ in) thick

sesame oil, for drizzling

400 g (14 oz) cascaval cheese

200 g (7 oz) halloumi

200 g (7 oz) kalamata olives, finely chopped

1 bunch of parsley, finely chopped

1 bunch of mint, finely chopped

3 garlic cloves, finely grated

50 ml (1¾ fl oz) passata (pureed tomatoes)

1 quantity of pita bread dough (page 154), 1 teaspoon crushed fennel seeds added to the dough

flour, for dusting

1 egg, beaten

To serve

100 g (3½ oz) feta

1 small red onion, cut into thin rounds

50 g (1¾ oz) roasted red peppers in oil (from a jar or your deli)

mint leaves, to garnish

parsley leaves, to garnish

Preheat the oven to 170°C (340°F). Line a baking tray with baking paper, spread the leek rounds on top and drizzle with sesame oil. Bake for 10 minutes, then remove from the oven.

Increase the oven temperature up to 220°C (430°F).

Grate the cascaval and halloumi into a bowl. Add the olives, parsley, mint, garlic and passata. Add the baked leek and mix together.

Divide the rested pide bread dough into six equal pieces. On a lightly floured work surface, roll out each piece with a rolling pin to form a circle about 2 cm (¾ in) thick.

Top each pide dough piece with one-sixth of the cheese mixture and fold the edges over the filling to create a small nest. Place on a lined baking tray and brush the dough with the beaten egg.

Bake for 7–10 minutes, until the bread is cooked and golden.

Remove from the oven and crumble the feta over each pide. Serve warm, garnished with the red onion, roasted peppers and a few mint and parsley leaves.

Note: *You can replace the halloumi and cascaval with a mixture of cheddar, gouda and emmental cheeses for a similar result. You can also drizzle some chilli oil over the pides!*

IBRIK

❋

NETTLE AND SPINACH PILAF
WITH YOGHURT

SERVES 6

1 tablespoon olive oil

1 white onion, sliced

300 g (10½ oz) wild rice

1 tablespoon white vinegar

120 g (4½ oz) spinach leaves,
  stems removed

18 nettle leaves (or spinach/chard)

75 ml (2½ fl oz) grapeseed oil

40 g (1½ oz) clarified butter, melted,
  or 50 g (1¾ oz) unsalted butter

2 tablespoons sweet paprika

50 g (⅓ cup) crushed salted almonds

1 tablespoon sultanas (golden raisins)

Spiced yoghurt

250 g (1 cup) goat's cheese yoghurt

2 tablespoons sweet paprika

Heat the olive oil in a saucepan over medium heat and saute the onion for a few minutes, until soft and translucent. Add the rice and saute for 1 minute.

Meanwhile, bring a kettle of 800 ml (27 fl oz) of water to the boil. Pour into the pan and cover. Turn the heat off and let the rice soak for 45 minutes.

While the rice soaks, add the vinegar to a bowl of cold water. Soak the spinach leaves for 1–2 minutes in the vinegar water to wash them. Remove the clean leaves from the bowl with a slotted spoon and drain on paper towel.

Put on a pair of gloves to handle the nettle leaves. Immerse them in the same vinegar water for 1–2 minutes to wash them. Remove them from the water and drain on paper towel.

Brush the nettle leaves with the grapeseed oil, season with salt, then place them flat on a microwaveable plate. Microwave the leaves for 2 minutes at 600W. Remove from the microwave and set aside to cool and form crispy chips.

If making your own clarified butter, melt the butter in a small saucepan over very low heat. Skim off the thin white film that appears on the surface. Continue cooking over very low heat for about 10 minutes, without stirring, to remove as much of this film as possible. Pour the butter through muslin (cheesecloth) or a clean thin tea towel and collect it in a small bowl.

When the rice has soaked for 45 minutes, drain the rice and place in a clean saucepan. Add the clarified butter, paprika, crushed almonds and sultanas, mixing well. Pour in 100 ml (3½ fl oz) of water and season to taste with salt and pepper. Add the spinach leaves, then cover and cook over medium heat for 4 minutes – the rice should be slightly crispy.

Combine the spiced yoghurt ingredients in a bowl and season with salt and pepper.

Serve the pilaf with the spiced yoghurt, garnished with the nettle chips.

Note: *Nettles can be gathered in forests, meadows or gardens. Choose the small leaves at the end of the stem, as they are more tender and less prone to disease. Pick them wearing thick gloves and snip them with a pair of scissors. If you have any doubts at all about their edibility, do not use them.*

LENTILS WITH ASPARAGUS AND MIZITHRA

SERVES 6

2 tablespoons olive oil

1 white onion, finely sliced

2 teaspoons sea salt

5 garlic cloves, quartered

350 g (12½ oz) small black lentils

250 g (9 oz) asparagus spears

130 g (4½ oz) butter

100 g (3½ oz) aged mizithra (or very dry goat's cheese), grated, plus 50 g (1¾ oz) shaved

1 tablespoon tahini

1 spring onion (scallion), finely chopped

½ bunch of parsley, finely chopped

Rustic bread (page 153), to serve (optional; omit to keep recipe gluten free)

Heat the olive oil in a saucepan over medium heat. Add the onion, sprinkle with the salt and saute for a few minutes, until soft and translucent. Stir in the garlic and lentils and saute for 1 minute. Add 1 litre (4 cups) of water, then cook over medium heat for 12 minutes.

Trim the woody ends off the asparagus stems. Cut off the tender tips and set them aside, then cut the remaining stems into rounds 1 cm (½ in) thick.

Mix the asparagus rounds and butter through the lentils and simmer for 5 minutes.

Add the grated mizithra and tahini and season with salt and pepper. Gently stir with a wooden spoon, until the lentils form a creamy risotto.

Serve topped with the fresh asparagus tips, shaved mizithra, spring onion and parsley. If desired, serve with rustic bread on the side.

OKRA STEW WITH
BROAD BEAN HUMMUS

SERVES 6

60 ml (¼ cup) white vinegar

550 g (1 lb 3 oz) okra

3 tablespoons olive oil

2 white onions, sliced

4 garlic cloves, halved

2 tablespoons paprika

70 g (2½ oz) tomato paste
   (concentrated puree)

50 ml (1¾ fl oz) white wine

500 g (1 lb 2 oz) tomatoes, peeled

4 carrots, chopped

60 g (2 oz) granulated sugar

1 teaspoon ground cardamom

½ teaspoon ground cinnamon

½ red bird's eye chilli, chopped

½ bunch of parsley, chopped

1 spring onion (scallion), finely diced

Pita bread (page 154), to serve
   (optional; omit to keep
   recipe gluten free)

Broad bean hummus

200 g (7 oz) broad (fava) beans

1 garlic clove

juice of ½ lemon

1 tablespoon tahini

400 ml (13½ fl oz) grapeseed oil

❀ ❧

Add 1 tablespoon of the vinegar to a bowl of cold water. Cut the tops off the okra and discard them. Soak the okra in the vinegary water for 1 hour.

Meanwhile, make a start on the broad bean hummus. Pour 2 litres (2 quarts) of water into a saucepan, add a sprinkling of salt and bring to the boil. Add the broad beans and blanch for 1 minute. Without turning off the heat, use a slotted spoon to remove the beans and immediately plunge them into a bowl of iced water to stop the cooking process. Set aside.

Add the remaining 3 tablespoons of vinegar to the boiling cooking water. Add the okra and cook for 12 minutes, then remove using a slotted spoon and set aside.

Heat 2 tablespoons of the olive oil in a saucepan over medium heat and saute the onion and garlic for a few minutes, until the onion is soft and translucent. Stir in the paprika and tomato paste until the bottom of the pan is nicely browned. Pour in the wine and stir to deglaze the pan, then add the peeled tomatoes, carrot and okra, reserving about 50 g (1¾ oz) of the okra for garnish.

Bring to the boil, then reduce the heat to low. Stir in the sugar, cardamom, cinnamon and chilli. Simmer, covered, for 30 minutes, until the okra is tender and the sauce has thickened. Season with salt and pepper to taste.

While the stew is cooking, slice the reserved okra. Heat the remaining olive oil in a frying pan over medium–high heat and saute the okra for 8–10 minutes, until slightly golden and tender.

Meanwhile, finish making the broad bean hummus. Peel the blanched broad beans and place in a food processor with the garlic, lemon juice, tahini and 200 ml (7 fl oz) of water. Slowly pulse in the grapeseed oil until combined. Season to taste.

Spread the hummus on serving plates and top with the okra stew. Garnish with the sauted okra and sprinkle with the parsley and spring onion. If desired, serve with pita bread.

CREAMY SPELT AND MUSHROOMS

SERVES 6

800 g (1 lb 12 oz) button mushrooms, halved
250 ml (1 cup) sunflower oil
8 garlic cloves
7 thyme sprigs
7 bay leaves
salt
250 g (9 oz) spelt
1 litre (4 cups) cream (35% fat)
1 teaspoon granulated sugar
1 teaspoon ground black pepper
1 tablespoon olive oil
1 onion, diced
25 g (1 oz) butter
150 g (5½ oz) chanterelles
150 g (5½ oz) shiitake mushrooms
Pickled red onions (page 136), to serve

✶

Preheat the oven to 170°C (340°F).

Place the button mushrooms in a large baking dish and drizzle with 150 ml (5 fl oz) of the sunflower oil.

Pour another 50 ml (1¾ fl oz) of the sunflower oil into a blender. Add four of the garlic cloves and 500 ml (2 cups) of water and pulse briefly. Drizzle the mixture over the mushrooms.

Scatter five thyme sprigs and five bay leaves over the mushrooms. Place the dish in the oven and bake for 15 minutes. Remove from the oven and discard the thyme and bay leaves.

Using a slotted spoon, transfer the mushrooms to a deep saucepan and set aside.

Carefully measure the mushroom cooking juices. Add water to bring the liquid to the amount indicated by the spelt packet instructions. Pour into a separate saucepan. Add a pinch of salt, then bring to the boil. Stir in the spelt and cook according to the packet instructions. Drain and set aside.

Crush three of the garlic cloves and add to the saucepan with the button mushrooms, along with the remaining two thyme sprigs and two bay leaves. Add the cream, sugar and pepper and season to taste with salt. Simmer for 40 minutes over low heat, then adjust the seasoning with more salt, as the mushrooms will absorb a lot of it.

Heat the olive oil in a saucepan and saute half the onion over medium heat for a few minutes, until soft and translucent. Add the drained spelt, along with two ladlefuls of the creamy mushroom mixture and a pinch of salt. Cook over low heat for 5–8 minutes until the spelt absorbs the cream.

Meanwhile, in a frying pan, heat the remaining 50 ml (1¾ fl oz) of the sunflower oil over medium heat. Add the butter and the remaining onion and sweat for a few minutes. Finely grate or chop the remaining garlic clove and add to the pan along with the chanterelles, shiitake mushrooms and a pinch of salt and pepper. Cook for 10 minutes, stirring regularly.

Serve the mushrooms on a bed of spelt, topped with pickled red onions.

Note: *The pickled red onions add a welcome acidity to this creamy dish. If you don't have any, use a few capers or finely chopped pickles.*

BARBECUED PORK SPARE RIBS

SERVES 6

2 tablespoons sea salt

1.3 kg (2 lb 14 oz) meaty pork
   spare ribs

3 small heads of broccoli, cut
   into florets

150 g (5½ oz) garlic salt

150 ml (5 fl oz) sunflower oil

Paprika baste

½ pomegranate

2 tablespoons sunflower oil

2 red onions, sliced

2 shallots, sliced

4 carrots, sliced

6 garlic cloves, sliced

1 red bird's eye chilli, sliced

150 g (5½ oz) sweet paprika

70 g (2½ oz) tomato paste
   (concentrated puree)

1 tablespoon muscovado sugar

500 ml (2 cups) meat stock (ideally
   beef or pork)

To serve

200 g (7 oz) salted almonds, chopped

½ bunch of parsley, chopped

½ bunch of coriander (cilantro),
   chopped

3 limes, quartered

To prepare the paprika baste, extract the seeds from the pomegranate half by tapping it lightly on its skin with a spatula. Remove any remaining white membrane from the seeds, as it is bitter.

Heat the sunflower oil in a saucepan over medium heat and saute the onion and shallot for a few minutes, until soft and translucent. Add the carrot and saute for 4 minutes, then stir in the garlic, chilli, paprika, tomato paste and sugar. Cook, stirring, for another 2 minutes, before adding the pomegranate seeds and stock. Simmer over low heat for 30 minutes, then remove from the heat. Using a food processor, blend the mixture until smooth, then set aside.

While the sauce is simmering, preheat your barbecue to low.

Salt the spare ribs, then spread half the paprika baste over the ribs.

Cook the ribs over indirect low heat – about 120°C (250°F) – on the barbecue, covered (see Note), for about 1½ hours, until the meat has browned and can be easily pierced with a knife.

Spread the remaining paprika baste over each side of the ribs, then cover again and cook for another 1½ hours, until the meat has shrunk back about 1 cm (½ in) at both ends of the bones and comes off easily.

If you don't have a barbecue, you can cook them in the oven. Place the ribs in a baking dish. Cover with foil and bake at 160°C (320°F) for 2½ hours, then uncover and bake briefly until crisp.

Remove the cooked ribs from the heat and leave to rest for 10 minutes before serving.

When the ribs are nearly done cooking, preheat the oven to 180°C (350°F).

Line a baking tray with baking paper, then arrange the broccoli florets on the tray. Season with the garlic salt, drizzle with the sunflower oil and bake for 20 minutes, or until tender and nicely roasted.

When ready to serve, cut the ribs into sections and brush them with any remaining paprika baste.

Arrange the ribs on a platter with the roasted broccoli and sprinkle with the almonds, parsley and coriander. Serve with the lime wedges.

Note: *If you are using barbecue without a cover, simply use a large roasting tin to cover the ribs while they cook.*

IBRIK

MITITEI (ĆEVAPČIĆI)

SERVES 6

6 allspice berries

1 teaspoon coriander seeds

2 tablespoons sweet paprika

1 tablespoon dried thyme

1 teaspoon ground black pepper

700 g (1 lb 9 oz) full-fat minced (ground) beef

150 g (5½ oz) minced (ground) pork, preferably from the belly or neck

150 g (5½ oz) minced (ground) lamb shoulder

250 ml (1 cup) bone broth (or sparkling water)

1 onion, finely grated

5 garlic cloves, finely grated

20 g (¾ oz) salt

1 teaspoon baking soda

1 tablespoon sunflower oil

Garlic sauce (optional)

2 garlic cloves, crushed

250 ml (1 cup) water

Using a mortar and pestle, grind the allspice berries, coriander seeds, paprika, thyme and pepper to a fine powder. Quickly saute the spices in a dry frying pan over medium heat to release their aromas. Remove from the heat.

In a bowl, combine the beef, pork and lamb. Add the toasted spices, along with the bone broth, onion, garlic, salt and baking soda. Mix together thoroughly, until you obtain a smooth paste. Cover with plastic wrap and refrigerate for at least 5 hours, to allow the flavours to infuse the meat.

About 30 minutes before cooking, preheat your barbecue to medium. Remove the mixture from the fridge and form into sausage-like shapes, weighing about 150 g (5½ oz) each.

Barbecue over indirect medium heat, turning regularly for 12–15 minutes, or until well browned and cooked through. (For even more flavourful sausages, combine the garlic sauce ingredients and drizzle this over the meat during cooking.)

If you don't have a barbecue, you can also cook the mititei on the stove. Heat the sunflower oil in a frying pan over high heat and cook the sausages for 5 minutes on each side, until deeply browned and slightly crisp.

Mititei is delicious with sweet and sour mustard, or in pita bread topped with zacuscă (page 26) and vegetables of your choice.

Note: *Every family has its own mititei or ćevapčići recipe. I've simplified this one to make it more accessible and easier to make at home. The secret lies primarily in the combination of meats: it's essential to use at least two. You can omit the pork if you would like, and instead increase the amount of beef.*

CHICKEN SOUVLAKI
WITH CARAMELISED FENNEL

SERVES 6

1.2 kg (2 lb 10 oz) boneless chicken
  thighs, cut into 2.5 cm (1 in) chunks
3 fennel bulbs
3 tablespoons olive oil
2 tablespoons honey
Tzatziki (page 22), to serve
Pita bread (page 154), to serve
  (optional; omit to keep
  recipe gluten free)

Yoghurt marinade
400 g (14 oz) Greek-style yoghurt
70 ml (2¼ fl oz) olive oil
4 garlic cloves, sliced into strips
1 shallot, sliced into strips
zest and juice of 1 lemon
3 tablespoons dried oregano

Souvlaki are also known
as kalamaki. If you visit
Athens, don't be surprised
if you receive a gyros if you
order a souvlaki.

Place all the yoghurt marinade ingredients in a freezer bag. Add
the chicken and season with salt and pepper. Seal the bag and mix
everything well, so the chicken is coated all over. Marinate in the fridge
for at least 1½ hours, or up to 4 hours, turning the bag occasionally.

About 1 hour before cooking the skewers, preheat the oven to 170°C
(340°F), and start caramelising the fennel.

Cut the fennel bulbs in half, then remove the tough, stringy parts with
a knife. Pour the olive oil and honey into a frying pan over low heat.
Add the fennel bulbs, flat side down, and cook for 12–15 minutes until
completely caramelised.

Place the caramelised fennel in a baking dish, cover with foil and bake
for 15 minutes. Remove the foil and bake for a further 15 minutes,
to brown the top. Remove from the oven and keep warm.

About 30 minutes before cooking the skewers, thread the marinated
chicken cubes onto skewers and rest them at room temperature. Preheat
your barbecue to medium.

Cook the chicken skewers on the barbecue grill over direct medium
heat for 10 minutes, turning now and then, until cooked through.
Alternatively, you could cook the skewers using a chargrill pan on
the stove.

Serve the chicken souvlaki with the caramelised fennel, tzatziki and,
if desired, pita bread.

COFFEE-GLAZED PRIME BEEF RIBS
WITH CARAMELISED FIGS AND RED CABBAGE

SERVES 6

1.2 kg (2 lb 10 oz) prime beef ribs
 (or sirloin)
½ red cabbage, cut into 6 wedges
olive oil, for coating and drizzling
3 garlic cloves, finely grated
18 figs
juice of 1 lemon

Marinade

1 red onion, diced
1 onion, diced
2 garlic cloves, finely grated
1 tablespoon ground coffee beans
200 ml (7 fl oz) espresso coffee
2 tablespoons worcestershire sauce
2 tablespoons balsamic vinegar
2 tablespoons brown sugar
2 tablespoons sweet and sour mustard
1 tablespoon dijon mustard
25 ml (¾ fl oz) olive oil
a good pinch of sea salt

Place all the marinade ingredients in a saucepan over low heat, mix together and leave to reduce for about 10 minutes, until the sugar has completely dissolved and the ingredients are combined. Remove from the heat.

Pour the marinade into a large bowl, add the beef ribs and mix to coat all over. Cover with plastic wrap, and marinate in the fridge for at least 3 hours.

At least 30 minutes before cooking the ribs, remove them from the fridge and bring to room temperature. Preheat your barbecue to high.

Coat the cabbage wedges with olive oil and garlic and sprinkle with salt and pepper. Cut the figs in half and sprinkle with the lemon juice. Wrap the figs and cabbage wedges together in foil or arrange in a cast-iron pan, uncovered.

When ready to cook, sear the marinated ribs over direct high heat for 4–6 minutes per side. Move the ribs over indirect high heat and cook for another 15–20 minutes; for medium-rare meat, the ribs will be cooked when the internal temperature reaches 52–58°C (130–132°F) when tested with a meat thermometer.

If you don't have a barbecue, heat a drizzle of olive oil in a frying pan over high heat. Sear the marinated ribs for 4–6 minutes per side, then roast in the oven at 160°C (320°F) for 15–20 minutes.

Meanwhile, place the foil or cast-iron pan with the figs and cabbage directly over the coals and cook for about 25 minutes, until the cabbage is tender and the figs are soft and syrupy; watch carefully as they cook, as the figs and cabbage can cook quickly. If you don't have a barbecue with charcoal, wrap the figs and cabbage in foil and bake at 180°C (350°F) for 25 minutes.

Let the ribs rest for 10 minutes, then serve with the caramelised figs and cabbage, drizzled with olive oil and sprinkled with salt.

LAMB CUTLETS WITH FRIED AND CANDIED SHALLOTS

SERVES 6

12 lamb cutlets

Marinade

2 onions, sliced
6 garlic cloves, finely grated
1 hot green chilli pepper, seeded
  and chopped
5 thyme sprigs
juice of 1 lemon
250 ml (1 cup) red wine
150 ml (5 fl oz) olive oil
1 tablespoon honey
1 tablespoon ground cumin
1 teaspoon sea salt
Pita bread (page 154), to serve
  (optional)

Candied shallots

40 g (1½ oz) butter
500 g (1 lb 2 oz) shallots
4 tablespoons runny honey
2 tablespoons red wine vinegar
zest of 1 orange
1 small piece of fresh ginger, grated

Fried shallots

4 shallots, finely chopped
150 g (1 cup) plain (all-purpose) flour
75 ml (2½ fl oz) sunflower or
  grapeseed oil

Place all the marinade ingredients in a very large freezer bag. Add the lamb cutlets, seal the bag and mix everything well, so the lamb is coated all over. Marinate in the fridge for at least 3 hours, turning the bag occasionally.

At least 30 minutes before cooking the cutlets, remove them from the fridge and bring to room temperature. Preheat your barbecue to high, and start cooking the shallots.

To prepare the candied shallots, melt the butter in a cast-iron skillet or frying pan over medium–low heat. Add the whole shallots and cook, stirring now and then, for about 10 minutes. Add the honey, vinegar, orange zest and ginger, and season generously with salt and pepper. Add a little freshly boiled water so that there is a 5 mm (¼ in) depth of water in the pan. Stir to deglaze the pan, then cook uncovered over very low heat for about 20 minutes, until all the liquid has evaporated, stirring regularly. Adjust the seasoning and set aside for serving.

To prepare the fried shallots, roll the finely chopped shallots in the flour. Heat the sunflower oil in a frying pan over medium heat until it begins to simmer. Add the shallots to the oil and fry for about 5 minutes. When they have a nice caramelised colour, remove them from the pan with a slotted spoon and drain them on a baking tray lined with paper towel.

Meanwhile, cook the lamb cutlets on the barbecue over direct high heat for 5–10 minutes, depending on their thickness and your desired level of pinkness. Alternatively, you could cook the cutlets using a chargrill pan on the stove.

Serve the lamb cutlets with the candied and fried shallots, and your choice of accompaniments, such as pita bread.

Note: *Whatever marinade you use for your meat, always use an acidic ingredient (vinegar, wine, lemon) – it will make the meat tender.*

IBRIK

BALKAN BURGERS

SERVES 6

6 slices thick-cut bacon

400 g (14 oz) halloumi, sliced into 1 cm (½ in) thick pieces

2 ripe tomatoes, sliced

Patties

900 g (2 lb) minced (ground) lamb (a mix of fatty and lean meat)

1 egg, beaten

1 red onion, diced

2 garlic cloves, finely grated

1 bunch of parsley, chopped

1 bunch of dill, chopped

1 tablespoon ground cumin

100 ml (3½ fl oz) white wine

Potato buns

2 large potatoes, peeled and diced

400 g (2⅔ cups) plain (all-purpose) flour, plus extra for dusting

30 g (¼ cup) cornflour (corn starch)

20 g (¾ oz) granulated sugar

1½ teaspoons dried yeast

2 teaspoons fine salt

40 g (1½ oz) softened butter

1 egg

Caramelised onions

1 tablespoon butter

1 tablespoon sunflower oil

4 onions, roughly chopped

2 teaspoons brown sugar

pinch of salt

dash of balsamic vinegar

Glaze

50 ml (1¾ fl oz) milk

1 egg

Place the patty ingredients in a large bowl, season with salt and pepper and mix together well. Cover and leave to rest in the fridge for at least 3 hours.

Meanwhile, prepare the dough for the potato buns. (If convenient, you can make the dough the day before.) Bring a saucepan of water to the boil. Cook the diced potatoes for about 10 minutes, until tender. Drain, reserving 120 ml (4 fl oz) of the cooking water, and mash the potatoes until smooth.

In a bowl, mix together the flour, cornflour, sugar, yeast and salt. Add the softened butter and mix thoroughly. Add the egg and the reserved potato cooking water and mix briefly, then mix in the mashed potatoes. Knead in the bowl for about 10 minutes until smooth, then cover with plastic wrap and let the dough rise in a warm, draft-free place for 2 hours, or overnight in the fridge.

Line a baking tray with baking paper.

On a floured work surface, punch down the dough to deflate it, then roll it out to a thickness of 2 cm (¾ in). Cut into six circles using an 8 cm (3¼ in) round cookie cutter, or divide the dough into six pieces and form balls with floured hands. Place on the baking tray, cover with plastic wrap and leave to rise for another 45 minutes, until doubled in size.

Meanwhile, caramelise the onions. In a frying pan, heat the butter and oil over medium–low heat. Add the onion and saute for 5 minutes. Add the sugar and salt. Without waiting for the onion to brown, add a drizzle of balsamic vinegar, then cover and cook over low heat for 25–30 minutes, until soft and lightly carmelised. Set aside.

Preheat your barbecue to medium–high.

When ready to bake the buns, preheat the oven to 170°C (340°F). Combine the glaze ingredients in a small bowl, brush the buns with the mixture and bake for 25 minutes.

Meanwhile, form the patty mixture into six even balls, about 200 g (7 oz) each, then flatten them with the palm of your hand. Let them rest at room temperature for 15 minutes before cooking.

On the barbecue, cook the patties over direct medium–high heat for 8–10 minutes. Alternatively, you could cook the patties using a chargrill pan on the stove.

Quickly sear the bacon and halloumi slices for 2–3 minutes per side, until golden and nicely grilled. Cut the potato buns in half and quickly toast the insides of the cut buns over low heat.

Place a patty on the bottom half of each bun, followed by the caramelised onion, halloumi, bacon and tomato slices. Top with the bun lids and serve immediately.

BARBECUED OCTOPUS

SERVES 6

2 fresh octopus, 600 g–1 kg
(1 lb 5 oz–2 lb 3 oz) each,
frozen for at least 24 hours

Poaching broth

750 ml (3 cups) red wine
3 carrots, roughly chopped
2 white onions, quartered
2 celery stalks, roughly chopped
2 bay leaves
2 rosemary sprigs
½ bunch of thyme
2 star anise
1 teaspoon juniper berries
1 tablespoon black peppercorns

Red pepper relish

5 red bell peppers (capsicums)
2 garlic cloves
1 tablespoon almond flour
1 tablespoon chopped walnuts
1 teaspoon sweet paprika
200 ml (7 fl oz) olive oil

Remove the octopus from the freezer and allow to thaw fully.

Place all the broth ingredients in a large deep saucepan. Pour in 5 litres (5 quarts) of water and bring to the boil. Carefully add the octopus, reduce the heat to low and cook for 45 minutes, or until the octopus is tender when pierced with the tip of a sharp knife.

While the octopus is simmering, make the red pepper relish. Grill the bell peppers on a barbecue (or in a chargrill pan on the stove) over direct high heat, until the skins are charred and the flesh is tender, making sure to turn them regularly. Transfer to a deep dish, cover with plastic wrap and leave at room temperature for 30 minutes.

Once the peppers have cooled, remove the skins, stems and seeds. Place the flesh in a food processor with the garlic, almond flour, walnuts and paprika and blend until smooth. With the motor running, slowly drizzle in the olive oil to emulsify the sauce.

When the octopus is tender, carefully remove it from the poaching broth, discarding the broth. Using a sharp knife, separate the tentacles from the head. (You won't be using the heads, but you can slice them thinly, refrigerate in an airtight container and serve them in a salad.)

Coat the tentacles with the relish, reserving extra for serving. Barbecue for 1½–2 minutes on each side over direct high heat, until nicely charred. Alternatively, you could cook them using a chargrill pan on the stove.

The octopus is lovely served with the extra relish, alongside dill and onion pilaf (page 87) and pickled red onion (page 136).

BARBECUED CORN

SERVES 6

50 g (1¾ oz) butter
1 thyme sprig
1 bay leaf
pinch of salt
6 corn cobs, husks removed

Dill and orange butter

100 g (3½ oz) softened butter
1 bunch of dill, chopped
zest of 1 orange

Place the butter, thyme sprig, bay leaf and salt in a large deep saucepan. Add 4 litres (4 quarts) of water and bring to the boil. Add the corn cobs and boil for 5 minutes.

Drain the corn cobs and shake vigorously to remove excess water.

Preheat your barbecue to medium.

Combine the dill and orange butter ingredients in a bowl.

Cook the corn cobs on the barbecue over direct medium heat for 10–15 minutes, turning regularly. (Alternatively, you could cook the corn using a chargrill pan.)

Generously brush the dill and orange butter all over the corn and serve hot.

POACHED SPICY SEA BREAM

SERVES 6

6 sea bream, about 300 g (10½ oz)
  each, gutted and trimmed
juice of 1 lemon
1 bunch of parsley, chopped

Poaching broth

4 onions, halved
6 tomatoes, halved
5 garlic cloves, sliced
2 hot green chillies, halved and
  seeded
2 tablespoons black peppercorns
2 tablespoons timut peppercorns or
  Sichuan peppercorns
1 tablespoon sweet paprika
3 tablespoons salt

Salsa

zest and juice of 1 lemon
4 garlic cloves
2 tablespoons fine salt
200 ml (7 fl oz) sunflower oil

Originally from Romania,
this simple dish will
delight seafood lovers
as its flavours are so
surprising and unique.

Start by making the broth. On a barbecue (or in a chargrill pan on the stove), sear the onions and tomatoes for 10 minutes over direct high heat, turning to create a thin crust on both sides. Place them in a saucepan that is wide and tall enough to accommodate all the fish. Add the remaining broth ingredients.

Pour in 6 litres (6 quarts) of water and bring to the boil, then simmer over low heat for 10 minutes.

While the broth is simmering, season the fish inside and out with salt and pepper. Sprinkle with the lemon juice. Sear the fish on the barbecue (or in a chargrill pan) over direct high heat for a maximum of 2 minutes on each side, or just until some beautiful sear lines appear.

Carefully place the grilled fish in the poaching broth and simmer over low heat for 5 minutes. Turn off the heat and let stand for 10 minutes.

To make the salsa, remove the tomatoes, onions and chillies from the poaching broth, reserving the broth, and place them in a food processor. Add the lemon zest, lemon juice, garlic and salt and blend until smooth. With the motor running, slowly drizzle in the sunflower oil until creamy and emulsified. Set aside in a serving bowl.

To serve, arrange the fish in a large deep-sided dish and cover with the poaching broth. Sprinkle with the chopped parsley and serve with the salsa.

Note: *The fish flesh is perfect when it takes on a light pearly colour, so be sure to monitor the cooking time carefully.*

»SIRELA« BJELOVAR
PODRAVEC
MASNI SIR BEZ KORE
DATUM PROIZVODNJE: 45 % MASTI U S.TV.

PRESERVES, PICKLES & CURED MEATS

WITH A CLIMATE THAT CAN SOMETIMES BE VERY HOSTILE, PRESERVATION HAS LONG OCCUPIED A VERY IMPORTANT PLACE IN BALKAN CULTURE – SO MUCH SO THAT IT DESERVES ITS OWN CHAPTER IN THIS BOOK.

Even with the advent of the refrigerator and freezer, we continue to salt, boil and smoke food because we like the flavours that these methods impart. Over time, we have cultivated a tradition of wasting nothing, of using every part: if not for food, then another purpose.

FERMENTED CABBAGE

MAKES 2 FERMENTED CABBAGES

2 green cabbages (see Notes)
2½ teaspoons untreated coarse salt
  per 1 litre (4 cups) water
1 tablespoon cumin seeds
4 sprigs of wild dill or fennel
  (see Notes)
1 bunch of dried thyme

Equipment

1 × 7 litre (7 quart) fermentation
  container with lid

Wash the cabbages thoroughly. Remove any damaged outer leaves and cut away the hard inner core.

Place both cabbages in your sterile fermentation container. Fill with cold water until they are completely submerged. Remove the cabbages from the water, measure the amount of water in the container, then weigh out 15 g (½ oz) coarse salt for every 1 litre (4 cups) water.

Dissolve the coarse salt in the water. Add half the cumin seeds, dill sprigs and thyme. Place the cabbages in the water. The cabbages will float in the water due to the salt: to submerge them, cover with a clean plate and place a clean heavy object on top. Add the remaining cumin seeds, dill and thyme, then close the container – but not too tightly, as you want to allow the fermentation gases to escape.

Let the mixture rest for 1 day in a cool place away from light (ideally in a cellar).

Daily for the next 7 days, open the container, remove the weight and plate, and stir the mixture with a large spatula, making sure to get to the bottom, to activate fermentation. Replace the plate and weight and loosely close the container each time and leave to ferment.

After 7 days, without removing the weight and plate, store the container in a cool, dark place for 2–3 months, after which time the cabbage will be ready to use.

You can enjoy the cabbage in salads, but it's best used to make sarma (page 59).

The cabbage will keep submerged in brine stored in the fridge for up to 6 months.

Notes: *Choose green, organic cabbages that are fairly large and have very thin leaves. You can also use white cabbage, but the leaves are less flavourful and will be more difficult to roll if making sarma.*

If you can't find wild dill, you can add an extra bunch of fresh dill. If using wild dill, ensure it is edible.

DILL PICKLES

MAKES 1 × 1.5 LITRE (6 CUP) JAR

3⅓ teaspoons untreated coarse salt
1 bunch of dill
3 sprigs of wild dill or wild fennel
  (see Notes)
2 garlic cloves
1 tablespoon mustard seeds
1 tablespoon black peppercorns
1 kg (2 lb 3 oz) small pickling
  cucumbers
1 horseradish root
½ hot green chilli, seeded and
  halved lengthways
1 celery stalk
1 dried thyme sprig

Equipment

1 × 1.5 litre (6 cup) preserving jar
  with a rubber seal lid

Pour 1.5 litres (6 cups) of water into a saucepan, add the salt and bring to the boil.

In the bottom of your sterile preserving jar, place ½ bunch of dill and two wild dill sprigs. Add half the garlic, mustard seeds and peppercorns. Add the cucumbers, making sure they are tightly packed, evenly distributing the horseradish and green chilli between each layer of cucumbers.

Pour the boiling brine over the pickles, ensuring they are completely submerged. Shake the jar to distribute the water evenly and remove any air bubbles. Top up, if necessary, with more boiling water to fill the jar within 2 cm (¾ in) of the rim.

Finish by adding the celery stalk and thyme sprig, and the remaining wild dill sprig, fresh dill, garlic, mustard seeds and peppercorns.

Close the lid tightly and turn it upside down. Leave it upside down for at least 12 hours, then store in a cool dark place (ideally a cellar). Leave to pickle for at least 2–3 months before using.

The pickles will keep submerged in brine for up to 6 months in the fridge.

Notes: *If you can't find wild dill, you can add an extra bunch of fresh dill. If using wild dill, ensure it is edible.*

The horseradish and chilli are essential as they help the pickles stay firm.

PICKLED RED ONIONS

MAKES 1 × 700 ML (23 FL OZ) JAR

3 red onions
1 teaspoon coriander seeds
1 teaspoon black peppercorns
½ bunch of dill
200 ml (7 fl oz) white vinegar
100 g (3½ oz) granulated sugar

Equipment
1 × 700 ml (23 fl oz) preserving jar
  with a rubber seal lid

❋ ⚜

Remove the seal from your jar, then place both in a large saucepan and fill with enough water to cover the jar. Bring the water to the boil, then leave to boil for 10 minutes to sterilise the jar and seal.

Cut the onions in half lengthways. Place on the chopping board, cut side down, then cut into thin strips.

Remove the jar and seal from the hot water. Once they are cool enough to handle, replace the seal.

Add the onion, coriander seeds, peppercorns and dill.

Put the vinegar and sugar in a saucepan, add 400 ml (14 fl oz) of water and bring to the boil. Pour the mixture into the jar, then close the lid tightly. Turn the jar upside down and leave to cool to room temperature.

Once cooled, store the pickled onion in the fridge and use within 1 month.

MUSTARD SEED PICKLES

MAKES 1 × 700 ML (23 FL OZ) JAR

300 g (10½ oz) mustard seeds
1 thyme sprig
1 bay leaf
300 ml (10 fl oz) white vinegar
300 g (10½ oz) granulated sugar

Equipment
1 × 700 ml (23 fl oz) preserving jar
  with a rubber seal lid

❋ ⚜

Fill a saucepan with water and bring to the boil. Add the mustard seeds and boil for 1 minute, then drain.

Add fresh water to the pan with the mustard seeds and bring back to the boil, then drain again.

Repeat this process two more times to remove the bitterness from the mustard seeds.

Meanwhile, place the jar and seal in a large saucepan and fill with enough water to cover the jar. Bring the water to the boil, then leave to boil for 10 minutes to sterilise the jar and seal. Once they are cool enough to handle, replace the seal.

Add the drained seeds, thyme sprig and bay leaf to the jar.

Put the vinegar and sugar in a saucepan, add 300 ml (10 fl oz) of water and bring to the boil. Pour the mixture into the jar, then close the lid tightly. Turn the jar upside down and leave to cool to room temperature.

Once cooled, store the pickled mustard seeds in the fridge and use within 1 month.

SPICY PICKLED ROASTED BEETROOT

MAKES 3 × 500 ML (2 CUP) JARS

1 kg (2 lb 3 oz) raw beetroot (beets)
2 tablespoons olive oil
1 teaspoon coarse salt
1 teaspoon ground black pepper

Marinade

80 g (2¾ oz) horseradish root
100 ml (3½ fl oz) sunflower oil
90 ml (3 fl oz) white vinegar
2 teaspoons coarse salt
2 teaspoons granulated sugar
juice of ½ lemon

Equipment

3 × 500 ml (2 cup) preserving jars
 with rubber seal lids

Preheat the oven to 200°C (400°F). Coat the beetroot with the olive oil, then sprinkle with the salt and pepper. Individually wrap each beetroot in foil and bake for 1–2 hours, until the centres are tender when pierced with a fork or the tip of a knife.

Remove from the oven, leaving the beetroot wrapped in foil, and leave to rest for 30 minutes at room temperature.

To prepare the marinade, peel the horseradish root and grate as finely as possible into a bowl. Add the sunflower oil, vinegar, salt, sugar and lemon juice and mix to combine.

Peel and thinly slice the beetroot, then add to the marinade, mixing gently to coat. Cover with plastic wrap and marinate in the fridge for at least 2 hours.

Divide the mixture between the three clean jars. Close the lids tightly, store in the fridge and use within 1 week.

PICKLED VEGETABLES
IN MUSTARD SAUCE

MAKES 3 × 500 ML (2 CUP) PRESERVING JARS

500 g (1 lb 2 oz) bell peppers (capsicums), cut into 2 cm (¾ in) cubes
350 g (12½ oz) carrots, sliced diagonally
350 g (12½ oz) onions, sliced
350 g (12½ oz) celeriac, grated
500 ml (2 cups) sunflower oil
300 g (10½ oz) wholegrain mustard
30 g (1 oz) pink peppercorns
5 bay leaves

Brine

500 ml (2 cups) distilled vinegar
350 g (12½ oz) granulated sugar
30 g (1 oz) sea salt

Equipment

3 × 500 ml (2 cup) preserving jars with rubber seal lids

Place the bell pepper and carrot in one bowl and the onion and celeriac in a second bowl. Sprinkle all the vegetables lightly with salt. Knead lightly to start softening them.

Combine the brine ingredients in a large saucepan, pour in 300 ml (10 fl oz) of water and bring to the boil.

Add the bell pepper and carrot to the brine and blanch for a maximum of 4 minutes, until they are tender but still firm and bright in colour. Remove with a slotted spoon and place in a large bowl. Blanch the onion and celeriac for just 1 minute, then remove with a slotted spoon and add to the bowl. Cover and refrigerate overnight.

Using a food processor, blend the sunflower oil and mustard until emulsified to a mayonnaise consistency. Pour the mustard sauce over the blanched vegetables, add the peppercorns and bay leaves and gently mix to combine. Cover with plastic wrap and refrigerate overnight.

The next day, remove the seals from your jars and place both seals and jars into a large saucepan. Fill with enough water to cover the jars. Bring the water to the boil, then leave to boil for 10 minutes to sterilise the jars and seals. Once they are cool enough to handle, replace the seals.

Fill the jars with the vegetable mixture and close the lids tightly.

Place the jars in a saucepan, upside down. Fill the saucepan three-quarters full with water, bring to the boil, then reduce to a simmer and cook for 30 minutes.

Remove the jars from the water and let sit for 2 hours.

Store in a cool dark place (ideally a cellar) and use within 2 months.

IBRIK

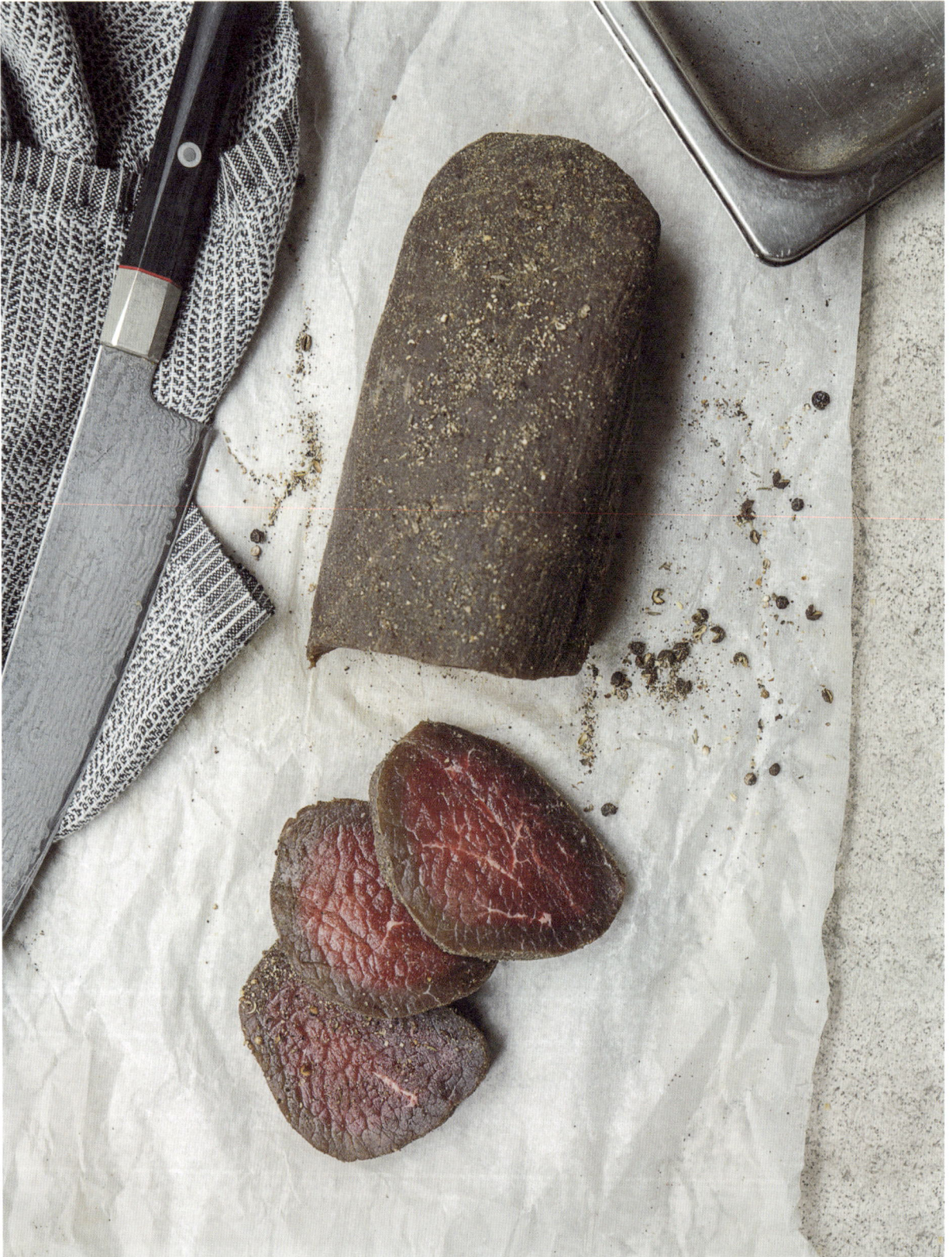

BEEF PASTRAMĂ

SERVES 6

500 g (1 lb 2 oz) coarse salt
1 × 400 g (14 oz) piece of topside
    (top round beef)
1 tablespoon ground black pepper
1 teaspoon smoked paprika
1 teaspoon herbes de Provence

Sprinkle a layer of the salt over the bottom of a ceramic dish just large enough to hold the beef. Place the beef in the dish and coat well all over with the remaining salt. Loosely cover with a tea towel and refrigerate the beef for 4–5 hours.

Brush the salt off the beef, rinse the beef quickly in cold water and dry thoroughly with paper towel. The flesh should have shrunk, and the excess blood should have seeped into the salt.

Using a mortar and pestle, crush the pepper, paprika and herbs together. Sprinkle the mixture all over the beef, kneading it in well.

Wrap the meat tightly in a clean tea towel or parchment paper and refrigerate for at least 48 hours, but no longer than 72 hours.

When ready to serve, carve the meat into very thin slices. Serve with truffle shavings in winter, and with pickles in summer.

The pastramă will keep in an airtight container in the fridge for up to 7 days.

Note: *The longer the meat rests, the better it will taste. If you see blood on the towel, rewrap the meat in a clean towel. If you have a smoker, you can also smoke the meat before serving, for even more flavour.*

PORK LOIN PASTRAMI

SERVES 6

2 garlic cloves, finely grated
½ red chilli, finely chopped
1 teaspoon dried thyme
1 teaspoon pink peppercorns
1 teaspoon black peppercorns
1 bay leaf
40 g (1½ oz) coarse salt
300 ml (10 fl oz) beer (see Notes)
1 kg (2 lb 3 oz) pork loin (see Notes)
Rustic bread (page 153), to serve
  (optional)

Spice mix
4 garlic cloves
6 coriander seeds
5 allspice berries
4 fennel seeds
1 teaspoon herbes de Provence
1 teaspoon sweet paprika
1 teaspoon smoked paprika
1 teaspoon ground black pepper
1 teaspoon salt

Pour 1 litre (4 cups) of water into a deep ceramic dish large enough to hold the entire piece of pork. Add the garlic and chilli.

Using a mortar and pestle, roughly crush the thyme, peppercorns and bay leaf, then add to the dish. Stir in the salt, then pour in the beer and mix to dissolve.

Place the pork in the brine, ensuring it's fully submerged. Cover with plastic wrap and marinate in the fridge for 2–3 days.

Remove the pork from the marinade, discarding the marinade. Pat the pork dry with paper towel, then roll it tightly into a log and tie it up using butchers' twine. Place the pork in a clean dish and refrigerate, uncovered, for 24 hours to dry the meat out.

The next day, preheat the oven to 90°C (195°F). Remove the pork from the dish. Fill a deep dish with water and place it in the oven. Place an oven rack just above the dish, then place the pork on the rack.

Depending on the thickness of the loin, bake for 1½–2½ hours, or until the meat is fully cooked through when pierced with a skewer or meat thermometer: the internal temperature should be 68°C (150°F). Remove from the oven.

Place the spice mix ingredients in a food processor and blend to a smooth paste.

While the pork is still hot, coat it all over with the spice mixture. Leave the pork to rest at room temperature for 2 hours, then cover loosely and rest again in the fridge for another 24 hours.

Carve the pastrami into very thin slices to serve with accompaniments of your choice, such as rustic bread and your preferred dipping sauce.

The pastrami will keep in the fridge in an airtight container for up to 5 days.

Notes: *A lighter flavoured beer, such as a lager, is recommended.*

Any red meat can be used to make pastrami – including lamb, which I find to be the most succulent. This recipe is also delicious when made with beef, using either a piece of topside (top round) or brisket.

WATERMELON RIND JAM

MAKES 6 × 500 ML (2 CUP) JARS

1 kg (2 lb 3 oz) watermelon rind,
  flesh scraped off
1 vanilla bean, split lengthways
2 star anise
1 kg (2 lb 3 oz) granulated sugar
1 tablespoon lemon juice
1 teaspoon fine salt

Equipment

6 × 500 ml (2 cup) preserving jars
  with rubber seal lids

❋ ⚘

Cut the rind into 3 cm (1¼ in) cubes. Place in a large saucepan.

Add the vanilla bean and star anise to the pan. Pour in 1.5 litres (6 cups) of cold water and bring to the boil. Let boil for about 20 minutes, until the rind is soft. Remove the rind using a slotted spoon and set aside in a bowl.

Add the sugar to the cooking water and stir quickly to dissolve. Bring back to the boil, then simmer for 30–40 minutes, until the mixture has the consistency of thick syrup.

Stir the rind into the syrup, along with the lemon juice and salt. Cook over low heat for 1 hour,

checking occasionally, until the mixture has the consistency of jelly and the rind is transparent.

Meanwhile, sterilise your jars (see instructions on page 140).

Fill the jars with the hot jam and close the lids tightly. Turn the jars upside down and leave to cool to room temperature.

Store in a cool dark place (ideally a cellar) and use within 1 year.

Note: *Only use watermelon rind that is in perfect condition, otherwise the jam risks spoiling.*

ROSEHIP JAM

MAKES 6 × 250-300 ML (8½-10 FL OZ) JARS

2 kg (4 lb 6 oz) fresh rosehips,
  thoroughly washed
splash of white vinegar
700 g (1 lb 9 oz) caster
  (superfine) sugar
juice of 1 lemon

Equipment

6 × 250–300 ml (8½–10 fl oz)
  preserving jars with rubber
  seal lids

❋ ⚘

Place the rosehips in a large bowl, cover with water diluted with the vinegar, and leave for 5 minutes. Drain and discard bruised or soft rosehips. Using a small sharp knife, remove the black blossom at the bottom of each.

Place the rosehips in a large saucepan. Pour in enough cold water to submerge them. Bring to the boil, then reduce to a simmer and leave for 1 hour, until soft and squishy. Remove from the heat and let cool for 10 minutes.

Without squeezing the water out of them, scoop the rosehips with a slotted spoon into a food processor. Pulse until a paste forms.

Set a fine-mesh strainer over a large bowl and push the paste

through until smooth. Gradually stir in 1–2 tablespoons of water until thin but not runny.

Tip into a very large saucepan and stir in the sugar and lemon juice. Over low heat, stir constantly until boiling. Reduce to a simmer and cook for 15 minutes. Remove from the heat and rest for 15 minutes.

Meanwhile, sterilise your jars (see instructions on page 140).

Fill the jars with the jam and close the lids tightly. Turn upside down and let cool.

Store in a cool dark place (ideally a cellar) and use within 1 year.

Note: *If picking rosehips, ensure they're edible. Wear gloves when handling as they can be prickly.*

BRÎNZĂ "TILSIT"

BRAȘOV

45% grăsime
Data fabricației

LEI
31 kg
N.I.
1727/71

INDUSTRIA LAPTELUI BRAȘOV

BREADS & BAKES

THE TASTE OF BREAD BAKED IN
A CHARCOAL-FIRED OVEN WILL
UNDOUBTEDLY REMAIN ONE OF
MY MOST CHERISHED MEMORIES –
ONE THAT BRINGS UP FEELINGS
THAT ARE DIFFICULT TO DESCRIBE.

A staple of the human diet, bread in all its forms has
been revered across cultures since time immemorial,
and the Balkans are no exception. While we are hardly
the undisputed specialists in this field, our breads
and pastries, like pita, have become more popular
in recent years. Follow this chapter's simple baking
instructions to the letter, arm yourself with the right
equipment and we guarantee good results when
making these recipes.

SHAWARMA BREAD

MAKES 6

25 g (1 oz) fresh yeast
500 g (1 lb 2 oz) bread flour or plain
   (all-purpose) flour, plus extra for
   dusting
60 ml (¼ cup) buttermilk
35 g (1¼ oz) unsalted butter, melted
1 teaspoon granulated sugar
2 teaspoons fine salt
vegetable oil, for greasing

Garlic butter

100 g (3½ oz) unsalted butter
1–2 tablespoons chopped parsley
1 garlic clove, crushed

❋

Place the yeast and 1 tablespoon of the flour in a small bowl. Mix in 100 ml (3½ fl oz) of lukewarm water (ideally 40°C/105°F). Let the starter rest next to a heat source (around 30°C/85°F) for about 15 minutes, or until it begins to foam.

In a large bowl, combine the remaining flour, buttermilk, melted butter, sugar and salt. Add the yeast mixture, then slowly mix in 140 ml (4½ fl oz) of lukewarm water, until the dough is smooth and no longer sticks to the bowl. Form into a ball.

Flour a work surface, and coat your hands with a little oil. Knead the dough by flattening it with the palm of your hand and folding it over. Continue this process until the dough is elastic.

Form the dough into a ball, place in a clean bowl and cover with a damp tea towel. Leave to rise at warm room temperature (around 25°C/75°F) for 30 minutes, until doubled in size.

Once it has risen, punch the dough to deflate it, then cut it into six equal portions and roll into balls. Place one ball on a lightly floured work surface. Using a rolling pin, slowly roll the dough out, from the centre outwards, regularly turning the dough a quarter turn to ensure an even thickness, until you have a circle about 25 cm (10 in) in diameter. Repeat with the remaining dough balls.

Combine the garlic butter ingredients in a small saucepan over low heat, stirring until melted and combined. Season with salt, remove from the heat and set aside.

To cook the shawarma bread, heat a large frying pan over high heat without oil. Place one of the dough circles in the hot pan and cook for about 30 seconds, or until bubbles begin to form on the surface. Turn the bread over and cook for another 1–2 minutes, until golden spots appear and the bread puffs slightly. Using a brush, spread some of the garlic butter over the entire surface, then transfer to a plate.

Cook the remaining dough in the same way and serve warm.

The bread is best served fresh, but will keep in an airtight container for 1–2 days.

RUSTIC BREAD

SERVES 6-8

10 g (¼ oz) fresh yeast

400 g (14 oz) plain (all-purpose) flour,
 plus extra for dusting

2 teaspoons fine salt

1 teaspoon granulated sugar

40 ml (1¼ fl oz) olive oil, plus extra
 for brushing and drizzling

1 tablespoon dried rosemary

1 tablespoon dried oregano

black and white sesame seeds,
 for sprinkling

✳

Place the yeast, flour, salt and sugar in a large bowl. Using a wooden spoon or spatula, mix in the olive oil and 200 ml (7 fl oz) of lukewarm water (ideally 40°C/105°F) until combined.

Turn the dough out onto a lightly floured work surface and knead for about 10 minutes, until elastic and smooth.

Return the dough to the bowl, cover with a damp tea towel and leave to rise at room temperature near a heat source (around 30°C/85°F) for 30 minutes, until doubled in size. Once risen, keep covered and refrigerate for 2 hours.

Generously brush a 22 cm (8¾ in)-long oval pan with olive oil.

Using a rolling pin, roll out the dough to fit the pan. Place the dough in the pan and sprinkle with the rosemary, oregano and sesame seeds. Cover with a damp teaa towel and let the bread rise at room temperature for a further 30 minutes.

Meanwhile, preheat the oven to 180°C (350°F).

Drizzle a little more olive oil over the bread, then bake for 15–20 minutes, or until golden and cooked through.

Best served warm, but also delicious cold.

The bread will keep in an airtight container for up to 2 days.

PITA BREAD

MAKES ABOUT 20

8 g (¼ oz) fresh yeast

900 g (2 lb) plain (all-purpose) flour, plus extra for dusting

100 ml (3½ fl oz) olive oil

1½ teaspoons fine salt

✳

Likely originating in Türkiye or Greece, pita bread is said to have given its name, through distortion, to the word 'pizza'.

Place the yeast and 1 tablespoon of the flour in a small bowl. Mix in 100 ml (3½ fl oz) of lukewarm water (ideally 40°C/105°F). Let the starter rest next to a heat source (around 30°C/85°F) for about 15 minutes, or until it begins to foam.

Place the remaining flour in a large bowl. Add the yeast mixture, olive oil and 400 ml (13½ fl oz) of lukewarm water and quickly mix until combined. Add the salt and, on a lightly floured surface, knead the dough for 7–10 minutes until it is firm and elastic.

Shape the dough into a ball. Lightly flour the mixing bowl and place the dough in it. Cover with a tea towel and let rest overnight in the fridge.

The next day, punch the dough down to deflate it, then form into balls of about 100–120 g (3½–4½ oz) each. Place them on a floured baking tray, cover with a damp tea towel and let rise in a warm place for about 1 hour, until doubled in size.

Preheat the oven to 220°C (430°F). Gently flatten the balls with your hands, then bake for about 20 minutes, until the pitas are puffed and golden.

The pitas will keep in an airtight container for up to 3 days.

Note: *Pita bread is delicious with mezze and barbecued dishes.*

GARLIC BRIOCHE

SERVES 6-8

335 ml (11½ fl oz) milk

20 g (¾ oz) fresh yeast

555 g (1 lb 4 oz) cake flour, plus
  extra for dusting

½ tablespoon fine salt

750 ml (3 cups) neutral-flavoured oil,
  plus extra for brushing and coating

1 tablespoon granulated sugar

olive oil, for brushing

1 teaspoon toasted sesame seeds
  (optional)

Garlic butter

100 g (3½ oz) unsalted butter, melted

3 garlic cloves, finely chopped

4 parsley sprigs, finely chopped

1 tablespoon fine salt

✻

In a small saucepan, gently heat the milk until it reaches 30°C (85°F); if you don't have a thermometer, it should be about body temperature when tested with a finger. Pour the hot milk into a bowl, add the yeast and 1 tablespoon of the flour and mix together. Let the starter rest next to a heat source (around 30°C/85°F) for about 15 minutes, or until it begins to foam.

Sift the remaining flour and salt into a large bowl. Add the yeast mixture, oil and sugar, gently mixing with a spatula until you have a reasonably smooth dough.

Lightly coat your hands and work surface with oil. Place the dough on the work surface and knead vigorously for about 15 minutes, until smooth and elastic.

Form the dough into a ball, place in a floured bowl, cover with plastic wrap and leave to rise at room temperature, near a heat source, for 45 minutes, until doubled in size.

Combine the garlic butter ingredients in a small bowl, cover with plastic wrap and leave to infuse.

Brush a small baking dish, about 18 cm (7 in) in diameter and 10 cm (4 in) deep, with olive oil. Once the dough has risen, cut out rounds using a 1–1.5 cm (½ in) cookie cutter and shape into small 1–2 cm (½–¾ in) balls. Place in the oiled dish, filling the dish with them. Leave to rise for another 30 minutes.

Preheat the oven to 180°C (350°F). Generously brush the garlic butter over the bread and, if desired, sprinkle the sesame seeds on top. Bake for 30 minutes, or until the top is golden brown and a knife inserted into the middle of the brioche comes out clean.

Remove from the oven, cover with a clean tea towel and let the bread rest for 15 minutes before serving.

The brioche is best served fresh, but will keep in an airtight container at room temperature for up to 2 days or in the fridge for up to 4 days.

CORNBREAD

SERVES 6-8

110 g (4 oz) butter, softened
50 g (1¾ oz) caster (superfine) sugar
2 eggs
235 ml (8 fl oz) buttermilk, at room
   temperature
140 g (5 oz) coarse cornmeal
140 g (5 oz) plain (all-purpose) flour,
   plus extra for dusting
20 g (¾ oz) cornflour (corn starch)
2 teaspoons fine salt
1¼ teaspoons baking powder
1 teaspoon baking soda
½ bunch of parsley, finely chopped
½ bunch of dill, finely chopped
vegetable oil, for brushing

✳

Preheat the oven to 170°C (340°F).

Place the butter and sugar in a large bowl and mix until smooth, using a spatula. Mix in the eggs, one at a time, until the mixture is perfectly smooth.

Mix in half the buttermilk, then pour in the rest and mix again.

Sift the cornmeal and flour into another bowl, along with the cornflour, salt, baking powder and baking soda. In three batches, mix the flour mixture through the batter, stirring between each addition. Finish by stirring in the parsley and dill.

Oil a 22 cm (8¾ in) loaf tin and dust with flour, shaking off the excess. Pour in the batter and smooth the top, then bake for 35 minutes, or until the top is golden brown and a knife inserted into the centre of the loaf comes out clean.

The cornbread will keep in an airtight container for up to 3 days.

Note: *Cornbread is generally eaten on its own as a snack, but you can also serve it as a side with saucy dishes.*

KOULOURI

MAKES 10

16 g (½ oz) fresh yeast
150 g (5½ oz) 00 flour
350 g (12½ oz) plain all-purpose flour
1½ teapoons fine salt
70 g (2½ oz) caster (superfine) sugar
vegetable oil, for greasing and brushing
60 ml (¼ cup) pomegranate molasses
100 g (⅔ cup) white sesame seeds
unsalted butter, at room temperature,
  for brushing

✳

Place the yeast in a large bowl. Whisk in 300 ml (10 fl oz) of lukewarm water until the yeast has dissolved. Let the starter rest next to a heat source (around 30°C/85°F) for about 15 minutes, or until it begins to foam.

Add the flours, salt and 35 g (1¼ oz) of the sugar, then mix in the bowl vigorously by hand for 20 minutes, or until you have a dough that is smooth, elastic and easy to handle; you can also use a stand mixer fitted with the hook attachment at medium speed.

Place the dough in a clean oiled bowl. Cover with plastic wrap and leave to rise at room temperature near a heat source for 1 hour, until doubled in size.

Preheat the oven to 200°C (400°F). Line two or three baking trays with baking paper.

Combine the molasses and remaining sugar in a bowl, pour in 500 ml (2 cups) of lukewarm water and mix to dissolve the sugar. Place the sesame seeds in another bowl.

Place the dough on an oiled work surface. Cut the dough into 10 equal pieces, weighing about 80 g (2¾ oz) each. Take one piece and, with your hands, roll to form a sausage shape about 20 cm (8 in) long, then join the two ends to form a circle. Repeat with the other dough pieces.

Quickly dip each circle in the molasses water, then in the sesame seeds, placing them on the lined baking trays.

Bake for 15–20 minutes, until golden brown. Remove from the oven and brush the koulouri with unsalted butter while they are still warm.

Serve with any type of cheese or with a spread.

The koulouri are best served fresh, but they will keep for 1 day in an airtight container.

GRÉGOIRE'S BABKA

SERVES 6

15 g (½ oz) fresh yeast
100 ml (3½ fl oz) milk
2 eggs, plus 1 yolk
1½ teaspoons fine salt
400 g (14 oz) plain (all-purpose) flour,
  plus extra for dusting
150 g (5½ oz) butter, softened
80 g (2¾ oz) granulated sugar

Chocolate spread

10 g (¼ oz) unsalted butter
40 g (1½ oz) dark chocolate
120 g (4½ oz) hazelnut-chocolate
  spread

Filling

20 g (¾ oz) candied orange peel, diced
40 g (¼ cup) crushed almonds

✳

IBRIK

Place the yeast, milk, eggs and salt in a large bowl and mix together using a wooden spoon.

Sift the flour and add it to the mixture a little at a time, mixing continuously. Knead the dough for about 5 minutes, until smooth. Gradually mix in the butter and sugar.

Place the dough on a floured work surface and knead again for about 15 minutes, until smooth, elastic and easy to handle. Transfer back to the bowl, cover with a damp tea towel and leave to rise at room temperature for 1 hour, until doubled in size.

Punch down the dough to deflate it, then place in a floured bowl. Cover with plastic wrap and refrigerate overnight.

The next day, prepare the chocolate spread. Melt the butter and chocolate together in a small saucepan over low heat. Stir in the hazelnut-chocolate spread until smooth, then remove from the heat.

Lightly flour your work surface. Divide the dough into three equal pieces, then roll each piece out into a 30 cm × 10 cm (12 in × 4 in) rectangle. Using a spatula, spread the chocolate mixture over each dough portion, then sprinkle evenly with the candied orange peel and crushed almonds.

Starting from the long side of one rectangle, roll up the dough tightly, then trim the ends to create a neat cylinder. Repeat with the other dough portions. Then, without cutting all the way through, use a sharp knife to make a deep cut lengthways in each cylinder, to reveal strips of filling.

Twist or braid the three cylinders together, then connect both ends of the dough together to create a wreath shape.

Line a baking tray with baking paper, then gently place the wreath on the baking tray. Leave to rise at room temperature for 1 hour.

Preheat the oven to 180°C (350°F).

To make the glaze, lightly whisk the egg yolk, then brush it over the brioche. Bake for 40 minutes, then check if the babka is cooked by piercing it with the tip of a knife: if it comes out dry, the babka is ready.

Remove from the oven and leave to cool for 30 minutes before serving.

The babka will keep in an airtight container for up to 3 days.

Note: *You can vary the filling by adding roasted and crushed hazelnuts, finely chopped Turkish delight, halva – whatever takes your fancy.*

TSOUREKI

SERVES 6

150 g (5½ oz) granulated sugar
35 g (1¼ oz) fresh yeast
1 teaspoon dried yeast
2 eggs, plus 1 yolk
85 ml (2¾ fl oz) evaporated milk
1 teaspoon ground cardamom
1 teaspoon mastic powder (optional)
1 teaspoon mahlab or ground
  cardamom
zest of 1 orange
seeds from 1 vanilla bean
1 teaspoon vegetable oil
1½ teaspoons fine salt
500 g (1 lb 2 oz) bread flour
75 g (2¾ oz) butter, melted

Glaze

400 g (14 oz) dark chocolate
  (60% cocoa), chopped
400 ml (13½ fl oz) cream (30–35% fat)

✳

In a small bowl, vigorously mix 1 tablespoon of the sugar with the fresh yeast until it becomes liquid, then stir in the dried yeast and 50 ml (1¾ fl oz) of lukewarm water. Let the starter rest next to a heat source (around 30°C/85°F) for about 15 minutes, or until it begins to foam.

In a large bowl, vigorously mix together the eggs, egg yolk and remaining sugar.

In a saucepan over low heat, gently heat the evaporated milk to 35°C (95°F); if you don't have a thermometer, it should be about body temperature when tested with a finger. Remove from the heat and stir in the spices, orange zest, vanilla seeds, oil and salt.

Pour the milk mixture over the egg mixture and stir again to incorporate. Now add the yeast mixture and 250 g (1⅔ cups) of the flour and mix in slowly. Gradually add the remaining flour, making sure not to overmix. When the batter is smooth, gradually pour in the melted butter while kneading slowly by hand, for about 20 minutes, until the dough is smooth, elastic and easy to handle; you can also use a stand mixer fitted with the hook attachment at low speed.

Cover the bowl with plastic wrap. Leave the dough to rise at room temperature near a heat source for 4 hours, until doubled in size.

Place the dough on a floured or oiled work surface and divide into three equal portions. Roll the dough pieces into rolls about 30 cm (1 ft) long and 3–4 cm (1¼–1½ in) thick. Braid the three rolls of dough together.

Line a baking dish with baking paper and place the braid on top. Cover with plastic wrap and leave to rest next to a heat source for at least 2 hours, until doubled in size; when pressed, the dough shouldn't spring fully back.

When the dough is nearly ready, preheat the oven to 170°C (340°F).

Bake the tsoureki for 40 minutes, or until it is golden brown and sounds hollow when tapped. Remove from the oven and leave to cool on a wire rack over a plate.

To make the glaze, set a heatproof bowl over a saucepan of simmering water, ensuring the bowl isn't sitting in the water. Add the chocolate to the bowl and melt over very low heat, then remove from the heat and immediately stir in the cream until the mixture is smooth, shiny and silky.

Pour the glaze over the cold tsoureki, coating it evenly, then leave to set. To speed up the glaze setting, you can place the tsoureki in the fridge.

Cut into slices to serve.

The tsoureki will keep in an airtight container for up to 3 days.

Note: *All ingredients should be at room temperature. Make sure the room temperature is warm and avoid breezes as much as possible.*

HADJI BEY'S

REAL GENUINE

HBC

TURKISH DELIGHT

RAHAT LOKOUM

ESTABLISHED IN CORK. 1902.

BE CAREFUL TO SEE THE NAME ON EACH LABEL H·B·C

IMITATIONS ARE DISAPPOINTING AND DO NOT PLEASE OR SELL AS WELL AS

HADJI BEY'S.

Largest Sale in Ireland.

FACTORY - MacCurtain St. CORK IRELAND.

DESSERTS

AMONG THE RICH CULINARY DIVERSITY IN THE BALKANS, DESSERTS HOLD A SPECIAL PLACE. IN A WAY, THEY TRULY REPRESENT THIS FABULOUS CULTURAL MELTING POT.

Firstly, because they are common to all the countries of the Balkan Peninsula, and secondly because every family has their own version, shaped by their particular local region and its waves of migration throughout the ages.

I firmly believe that culture is meant to be shared, and that introducing others to our heritage is the most effective way to preserve our traditions. The more these recipes are written down, the greater their reach will be.

BALKAN CHEESECAKE

IBRIK

SERVES 6

Crust

200 g (7 oz) plain (all-purpose) flour,
  plus extra for dusting
45 g (1½ oz) icing (confectioners')
  sugar
125 g (½ cup) butter, chilled
150 g (5½ oz) crepes dentelles or
  crispy wafers, crushed
seeds from 1 vanilla bean
zest of 1 lemon
1 egg, plus 1 yolk
1 tablespoon creme fraiche
pinch of fine salt

Filling

400 g (14 oz) cream cheese, at room
  temperature
200 g (7 oz) granulated sugar
360 g (12½ oz) creme fraiche
100 g (3½ oz) Greek-style yoghurt
4 egg yolks, at room temperature,
  beaten
juice of ½ lemon
40 g (⅓ cup) cornflour (corn starch)
200 ml (7 fl oz) double (heavy) cream
100 g (⅔ cup) white chocolate, chopped
seeds from 2 vanilla beans

Cherry coulis

200 g (1 cup) cherries, pitted and
  halved
2 tablespoons granulated sugar

✳

> This cheesecake would
> have fit just as well in the
> breads and bakes chapter.
> Indeed, traditionally, the
> cake looks more like a
> brioche filled with cheese.

To make the crust, sift the flour and icing sugar into a bowl. Cut the butter into 1 cm (½ in) cubes, then use a fork to cut the butter into the flour mixture until almost incorporated. Add the crepes dentelles to the bowl with the remaining crust ingredients and mix until you have a smooth dough. Form into a ball, cover the bowl with plastic wrap, then let the dough rest for 1 hour in the fridge.

Preheat the oven to 180°C (350°F).

On a floured surface, roll the dough out to a thickness of 1 cm (½ in) using a rolling pin. Place the dough in the bottom of a 20 cm (8 in) springform cake tin and trim any excess dough with a knife; if using a non-springform tin, line it with parchment paper first. Using a fork, prick the dough all over, so it doesn't bubble or shrink during baking.

Bake for 20 minutes, then remove from the oven, but keep the oven on.

While the crust is baking, make the filling. Set a heatproof bowl over a saucepan of simmering water, ensuring the bowl isn't sitting in the water. Add the cream cheese and sugar and whisk until smooth. Remove from the heat and set aside.

In another bowl, mix the creme fraiche and yoghurt with a spatula until combined. Using a whisk, fold in the beaten egg yolks in three batches. Once smooth, add the lemon juice and cornflour.

In a saucepan, warm the cream over medium heat until steam is rising but no bubbles have formed. Add the white chocolate and vanilla seeds, turn off the heat and stir until the chocolate has melted.

Pour the cream cheese mixture into the saucepan and mix well with a whisk. Finally, pour in the yoghurt mixture and mix with a spatula to maintain a light, airy texture.

Pour the cream mixture into the cooled crust. Fill a roasting tin with water to a depth of 3 cm (1¼ in) of water, then place the cake tin in the water bath. Transfer to the oven and bake at 180°C (350°F) for 30–35 minutes, until the top is golden brown.

Remove the dish from the oven, then remove the cake tin from the water bath. Leave to cool, then loosely cover and refrigerate for 4 hours, until set.

To make the coulis, place the cherries and sugar in a saucepan, add 3 tablespoons of water and simmer for 5 minutes, or until the cherries are soft. Let cool slightly, then pour the mixture into a food processor and blend for about 2 minutes; if desired, reserve a small portion of the softened cherries for decoration. Strain the mixture through a fine-mesh sieve to obtain a smooth liquid.

Serve the cake drizzled with the coulis and topped with the reserved cherries, if using.

The cake will keep covered in the fridge for up to 3 days.

FROMAGE FRAIS FRITTERS

SERVES 6

150 g (1 cup) plain (all-purpose) flour,
 plus extra for dusting
1 teaspoon baking powder
1 egg
50 g (1¾ oz) caster (superfine) sugar
250 g (1 cup) fromage frais (or ricotta),
 at room temperature
zest of 1 lemon
30 g (¼ cup) icing (confectioners')
 sugar
1 litre (4 cups) sunflower oil
400 g (14 oz) creme fraiche
200 g (7 oz) raspberry jam
poppy seeds, for sprinkling

✳

Sift the flour and baking powder into a bowl.

In another bowl, vigorously whisk together the egg and caster sugar, then mix in the fromage frais and lemon zest until combined. Using a spatula, fold in the sifted flour mixture and mix until smooth.

Cover the bowl with plastic wrap and refrigerate for 1 hour.

Dust your hands with flour, then form the dough into small 2 cm (¾ in) balls. Place them on a baking tray lined with baking paper.

Place the icing sugar in a bowl.

In a saucepan with sides deep enough to avoid risk of splashing or boiling over, heat the sunflower oil to 180°C (350°F), or until a cube of bread dropped in the oil browns in 15 seconds. Using a slotted spoon, gently lower a batch of dough balls into the hot oil and fry for 5–6 minutes, until golden brown. Scoop the fritters straight into the bowl of icing sugar and shake the bowl to evenly coat them in the sugar.

Repeat with the remaining dough balls, making sure not to crowd them in the oil.

To serve, divide the creme fraiche among serving bowls and place the hot fritters on top. Drizzle generously with the raspberry jam, sprinkle with poppy seeds and enjoy warm.

Note: *There's no need to work the dough too much, or the fritters might become tough when fried. Just mix enough to incorporate all the dough ingredients.*

DESSERTS

HALVA COOKIES

IBRIK

MAKES 12-18

500 g (1 lb 2 oz) butter, softened
400 g (14 oz) brown sugar
300 g (10½ oz) caster (superfine)
  sugar
3 large eggs
700 g (1 lb 9 oz) plain (all-purpose)
  flour
1½ teaspoons baking soda
1 teaspoon fine salt
150 g (1 cup) dark chocolate
  (70% cocoa)
30 g (1 oz) vanilla halva

❋

In a bowl, gently whisk the butter and sugars together. Add the eggs one at a time, incorporating them without overmixing. Gather the mixture together in the centre of the bowl between each egg.

Sift together the flour, baking soda and salt. Add to the egg mixture in two batches, mixing with a spatula until fully incorporated.

Roughly crush the chocolate and halva into chips, then add them to the cookie dough and mix briefly.

Cover the bowl with plastic wrap and refrigerate overnight, or freeze for 2 hours.

When ready to bake, preheat the oven to 170°C (340°F). Line a baking tray with baking paper.

Shape the dough into 100 g (3½ oz) balls and place on the lined baking tray. Bake for 10–12 minutes, or until the edge of the cookies are golden and a knife inserted in the middle of one comes out clean.

Remove from the oven and leave to cool.

The cookies will keep in an airtight container for up to 5 days.

Note: *To ensure successful cookies every time, don't overmix the ingredients.*

BALKAN MACARONS

DESSERTS

MAKES 12-14

4 egg whites
120 g (4½ oz) icing (confectioners')
  sugar
150 g (5½ oz) walnut meal
150 g (5½ oz) almond meal
zest of 2 limes

Preheat the oven to 180°C (350°F). Line a baking tray with baking paper.

Set a heatproof bowl over a saucepan of simmering water, ensuring the bowl isn't sitting in the water. Add the egg whites and whisk over medium heat until stiff peaks form. Turn off the heat and allow the egg whites to stand for about 2 minutes. Check with your finger: the whites should be lukewarm.

Take the bowl off the pan. Add half the sugar and continue whisking until smooth and still lukewarm. Whisk in the remaining sugar until the meringue has cooled completely.

Transfer the meringue to a clean bowl.

In a separate bowl, mix together the walnut meal, almond meal and lime zest until well combined. Working in two batches, slowly pour the mixture over the meringue, folding with a spatula in a circular motion, rotating the bowl to avoid crushing the meringue or knocking the air out.

Fit a piping bag with a 9 mm (½ in) nozzle and fill it with the meringue mixture. Pipe 4 cm (1½ in) macarons onto the lined baking tray.

Reduce the oven temperature to 120°C (250°F). Leaving the oven door ajar, bake the macarons for 5 minutes, then close the oven door and continue baking for 20 minutes.

Remove the macarons from the oven and leave to cool. These little cookies go perfectly with a cup of tea or coffee.

The macarons will keep in an airtight container for up to 4 days.

MORE THAN CHOCOLATE
FONDANT CAKE

SERVES 6-8

200 g (7 oz) unsalted butter, plus extra
  for greasing
2 tablespoons cornflour (corn starch),
  plus extra for dusting
200 g (7 oz) dark chocolate
  (64% cocoa), chopped
150 g (5½ oz) granulated sugar
4 eggs
2 teaspoons ground ginger
pinch of fine salt
ice cream, to serve (optional)
chocolate shavings, to serve (optional)

Preheat the oven to 170°C (340°F). Butter a 25 cm (10 in) cake tin and dust with cornflour, shaking off any excess.

In a saucepan, gently melt the butter and chocolate over very low heat.

Pour the mixture into a bowl. Add the sugar and whisk vigorously to combine, then leave to cool until lukewarm.

Whisk in the eggs, one by one, until smooth.

Sift the cornflour over the batter, then the ginger and salt, and mix again until smooth.

Pour the batter into the cake tin and bake for 25 minutes, or until a thin crust has formed but the centre is still gooey.

Remove from the oven and leave the cake to cool in the tin. It is best enjoyed at room temperature, served with a scoop of ice cream and chocolate shavings.

The cake will keep in an airtight container in the fridge for up to 3 days.

Note: *At the end of baking, you'll feel like the centre of the fondant cake is still undercooked. This is the desired effect!*

BAKLAVA

SERVES 6-8

280 g (10 oz) clarified butter, melted,
  or 350 g (12½ oz) unsalted butter
2 egg whites
400 g (14 oz) pistachio meal
1 tablespoon natural almond extract
8 cloves

Filo pastry

550 g (1 lb 3 oz) plain (all-purpose)
  flour
1 egg
1 tablespoon white vinegar
1 tablespoon lemon juice
cornflour (corn starch), for dusting

Syrup

200 g (7 oz) muscovado sugar
60 ml (¼ cup) honey
1 teaspoon rosewater

To prepare the filo pastry, place the flour in a large bowl with the egg, vinegar and lemon juice. Add 175 ml (6 fl oz) of room temperature water and mix until smooth.

Turn the dough out onto a work surface lightly dusted with cornflour and knead with the palms of your hands for about 10 minutes, until smooth. Form into a ball, return to the bowl, cover with a damp tea towel and leave to rest at room temperature for 20 minutes.

Meanwhile, if making your own clarified butter, melt the butter in a small saucepan over very low heat. Skim off the thin white film that appears on the surface. Continue cooking over very low heat for 10 minutes, without stirring, to remove as much of this film as possible. Pour the butter through muslin (cheesecloth) or a clean thin tea towel and collect it in a small bowl.

Divide the dough into four portions, then shape each piece into a log about 30 cm (1 ft) long and 3–4 cm (1¼–1½ in) thick. Cut each log into 10 pieces, roll into balls, then cover with a damp tea towel to keep moist.

Sprinkle a little cornflour on your work surface and rolling pin. One at a time, roll the balls of dough out as thinly as possible; you should be able to see through them. Sprinkle each sheet with a little cornflour, to prevent them sticking together, place on a plate and cover with a damp tea towel.

Preheat the oven to 180°C (350°F).

Beat the egg whites in a clean bowl until stiff peaks form. Using a spatula, gradually fold in the pistachio meal and almond extract.

Line a 24 cm (9½ in) round baking dish with baking paper. Brush both sides of a pastry sheet with the clarified butter, then place it in the dish. Repeat with another 19 filo pastry sheets, layering them. Using a spatula, spread the pistachio meringue over the top sheet. Butter both sides of the remaining 20 sheets, and layer them on top.

Using a sharp knife, cut the baklava into 3 cm (1¼ in) diamond shapes, fully slicing through the layers. Arrange the cloves on top.

Transfer to the oven and bake for 40 minutes, or until the pastry is deep golden and crisp.

Shortly before the baklava finishes baking, place the syrup ingredients in a saucepan with 100 ml (3½ fl oz) of water. Bring to the boil. Reduce to a simmer and cook, stirring, for about 2 minutes, until a smooth syrup.

Evenly pour the syrup over the baked baklava. Allow to cool completely before serving.

The baklava will keep in an airtight container for up to 7 days.

Note: *Better pistachio meal means better baklava. Make your own by lighlty roasting good-quality shelled, unsalted pistachios in the oven, letting them cool completely, then chopping them in a food processor.*

IBRIK'S CARROT CAKE

SERVES 6-8

butter, for greasing
200 g (7 oz) brown sugar, plus extra
  for dusting
2 eggs
pinch of fine salt
200 ml (7 fl oz) sunflower oil
zest of 1 orange
220 g (8 oz) plain (all-purpose) flour
2¼ teaspoons baking powder
1½ teaspoons ground cinnamon
250 g (9 oz) carrots, peeled and grated
30 g (1 oz) raisins
handful of pecans, lightly toasted
  (see Note)

Icing

40 g (1½ oz) unsalted butter
175 g (6 oz) cream cheese
150 g (5½ oz) icing (confectioners')
  sugar
seeds from 1 vanilla bean
zest of 1 orange, plus extra to garnish

❋

Preheat the oven to 170°C (340°F). Butter an 18 cm (7 in) loaf tin and dust with sugar, shaking off any excess.

Crack the eggs into the bowl of a stand mixer fitted with the whisk attachment, then add the brown sugar and salt and beat for 3–5 minutes at medium–high speed until pale and foamy. Add the sunflower oil and orange zest and mix to combine.

In another bowl, mix together the flour, baking powder and cinnamon. Sift over the batter mixture and mix until completely smooth. Stir in the carrots and raisins.

Pour the batter into the loaf tin and bake for 40 minutes, or until a knife inserted in the middle comes out clean and dry.

Remove from the oven and leave to cool in the tin.

To make the icing, gently melt the butter in a small saucepan over very low heat. Pour into a bowl, then add the cream cheese, icing sugar, vanilla seeds and orange zest. Mix together until you have a smooth, even and firm paste. If the icing is too runny, refrigerate for 15 minutes to firm it up.

To remove the cooled cake from the tin, run a knife around the cake's edges and flip it onto a plate.

Spread the icing over the cake. Chop up some of the pecans and sprinkle them on top, along with the extra orange zest.

The cake will keep in an airtight container in the fridge for up to 4 days.

Notes: *You can toast the pecans in the oven for 10 minutes while the cake is baking.*

IBRIK

IBRIK'S GRANOLA

SERVES 6

100 g (3½ oz) pecans
100 g (3½ oz) hazelnuts
100 g (3½ oz) dates, finely chopped
100 g (3½ oz) soft dried figs, finely
  chopped
100 g (3½ oz) raisins, finely chopped
170 g (6 oz) rolled oats
150 ml (5 fl oz) runny honey
100 g (3½ oz) brown sugar
65 ml (2¼ fl oz) sesame oil
65 ml (2¼ fl oz) coconut oil

Preheat the oven to 180°C (350°F).

On a baking tray lined with baking paper, spread the pecans and hazelnuts. Toast them in the oven for 10–15 minutes, until fragrant and golden brown. Remove the nuts from the oven and leave to cool, but keep the oven heated.

Place the dates, figs and raisins in a large bowl. Finely chop the cooled toasted pecans and hazelnuts and add to the bowl.

In a dry frying pan over medium–low heat, toast the oats, stirring regularly, for 5 minutes. Reduce the heat if the oats start to brown. Tip them into the bowl with the chopped nuts and fruit.

Now add the honey, sugar, sesame oil and coconut oil to the pan. Reduce the heat and simmer, stirring constantly, until the sugar and honey have dissolved and combined with the oil. Take off the heat and allow to cool for 5 minutes, then pour over the granola ingredients, stirring until completely combined.

Line a baking dish with baking paper. Spread the granola in the dish, to a thickness of about 3 cm (1¼ in).

Bake for 25 minutes, then remove from the oven. The granola will still be soft to the touch, but it will harden as it cools.

You can crumble the cold granola into large chunks to enjoy as a bar, or serve with Greek-style yoghurt and fruit.

The granola will keep in an airtight container in the pantry for up to 1 month.

DESSERTS

PORTOKALOPITA

SERVES 6

300 g (10½ oz) Greek-style yoghurt
4 large eggs
200 g (7 oz) caster (superfine) sugar
zest of 3 oranges
seeds from 1 vanilla bean
1 tablespoon baking powder
1 teaspoon ground ginger
pinch of fine salt
200 ml (7 fl oz) sunflower oil, plus
   extra for greasing
400 g (14 oz) filo pastry, chopped
   into very small pieces (see Notes)
orange slices, to serve (see Notes)

Orange syrup

2 oranges
2 lemons
400 g (14 oz) granulated sugar
2 cinnamon sticks
2 star anise

✳

Line a colander with muslin (cheesecloth) or a clean thin tea towel. Place the colander over a bowl, pour the yoghurt into it and cover. Let the yoghurt drain in the fridge for at least 1 hour to remove the excess liquid.

In a bowl, vigorously whisk the eggs and sugar. Stir in the drained yoghurt, orange zest, vanilla seeds, baking powder, ginger, salt and oil and mix until smooth.

Fold the filo pastry pieces into the batter. Let rest for 20 minutes to allow the pastry to soften and absorb the liquid, stirring occasionally to ensure even absorption.

Meanwhile, preheat the oven to 170°C (340°F). Grease a 42 cm (16½ in) cake tin.

Pour the batter into the cake tin and bake for 45 minutes, or until a knife inserted in the middle comes out clean and dry.

Meanwhile, make the orange syrup. Carefully slice the peel from the oranges, leaving behind any white pith on the flesh. Place the peel strips in a small saucepan. Squeeze the juice from the oranges and lemons and add to the pan. Add the sugar, cinnamon sticks, star anise and 500 ml (2 cups) of water, then bring to a simmer over medium–low heat. Once simmering, remove from the heat and leave to steep for at least 15 minutes.

Remove the cake from the oven and leave to cool for 5 minutes. To remove from the tin, run a knife around the cake's edge and flip onto a plate.

Use a knife to make small, invisible cuts in the cake. Spread the syrup over the top to soak into the cuts. Garnish the cake with orange slices, if desired, and cut into slices to serve.

The portokalopita will keep in an airtight container in the fridge for up to 3 days.

Notes: *Feel free to separate the filo pastry sheets before cutting them. The pastry pieces must be perfectly airy and not clump together.*

You can lightly roast your orange slices, or candy them; simply simmer the slices in equal parts water and sugar (1:1 ratio) for 30–40 minutes, until translucent.

APPLE PIE

SERVES 6

oil, for greasing
1 egg, beaten
icing (confectioners') sugar, for
  sprinkling

Pastry

125 g (½ cup) butter, melted
65 g (2¼ oz) creme fraiche
60 g (½ cup) icing (confectioners')
  sugar
1 egg, plus one yolk
zest of 1 lemon
pinch of fine salt
250 g (9 oz) plain (all-purpose) flour

Filling

1 kg (2 lb 3 oz) sweet but tangy apples
150 g (5½ oz) butter, melted
100 g (3½ oz) granulated sugar
60 g (½ cup) roasted walnuts, finely
  chopped
small handful of raisins
seeds from 1 vanilla bean
zest of 1 lemon
1 tablespoon dark rum
1 tablespoon ground cinnamon
pinch of sea salt

✳

To make the pastry, place the melted butter in a bowl with the creme fraiche, icing sugar, egg, egg yolk, lemon zest and salt. Mix by hand until combined, or mix using a stand mixer fitted with the paddle attachment at low speed. Add half the flour, stirring quickly, or at low speed if using a stand mixer, until combined. Add the remaining flour and mix again, avoiding overmixing as the dough will become tough. Cover the bowl with plastic wrap and leave to rest at room temperature for 1 hour.

Preheat the oven to 150°C (300°F).

To make the filling, grate the apples, including the skin, and place in a colander to drain for 20–30 minutes.

Transfer the grated apple to a large bowl. Add the remaining filling ingredients and combine using a spatula. Cover with plastic wrap and set aside at room temperature.

Place the dough on an oiled work surface, divide into two equal portions and shape into balls.

Grease a 24 cm (9½ in) pie dish. Roll one ball of dough out using a rolling pin, to cover the base and sides of the dish. Ease the dough into the dish, prick the dough a few times with a fork, then bake for 7 minutes.

Meanwhile, roll out the second ball of dough to fit the top of the pie dish.

Remove the pie dish from the oven. Increase the oven temperature to 170°C (340°F), and let the pie base cool slightly.

Spread the apple filling over the pie base, then place the pie lid on top. Pinch the pastry edges together, then brush the beaten egg over the top.

Bake the pie for a further 45 minutes, until it is golden brown on top.

Remove from the oven and allow to cool, then sprinkle with icing sugar.

The pie will keep in an airtight container in the fridge for up to 2 days.

STRAWBERRY COLIVĂ

SERVES 6

200 g (7 oz) pearl barley
200 g (7 oz) roasted walnuts, chopped
120 g (4½ oz) granulated sugar
zest of 1 lemon
zest of 1 orange
1 teaspoon rum (or rum essence)
seeds from 1 vanilla bean
pinch of fine salt
sliced strawberries, to garnish
lemon zest, for sprinkling

Strawberry coulis

200 g (7 oz) strawberries
zest and juice of 1 lemon

I hesitated for a long time before sharing this recipe, because it's generally made to honour a loved one who has passed away. It is made within 40 days of their death, and is one of our most profound rituals. But I offer this recipe as a form of homage that, I hope, won't shock my fellow Balkans.

Place the pearl barley in a bowl and rinse it three or more times with cold water to remove the excess starch. Drain well.

Place the pearl barley in a saucepan with 900 ml (30½ fl oz) of water. Cook over high heat for 45–50 minutes, until the water is absorbed and the barley grains are tender. Transfer to a bowl and leave to cool, then cover with plastic wrap and chill in the fridge overnight.

The next day, prepare the coulis. Hull the strawberries. Place in a food processor with the lemon zest, lemon juice and 50 ml (1¾ fl oz) of water. Blend for 2 minutes to emulsify, then transfer to a bowl, cover and refrigerate for 1 hour.

Meanwhile, mix the pearl barley with the walnuts, sugar, lemon zest, orange zest, rum, vanilla seeds and salt. Cover again and leave in the fridge for another 30 minutes to absorb the sugar.

Divide the pearl barley mixture among serving bowls. Drizzle with the coulis and serve garnished with fresh strawberries and lemon zest.

The colivă will keep in an airtight container in the fridge for up to 2 days.

MY CREME CARAMEL

SERVES 6

1 litre (4 cups) milk
1 star anise
1 cinnamon stick
seeds from 1 vanilla bean
pinch of fine salt
8 eggs
150 g (5½ oz) caster (superfine) sugar
100 g (⅔ cup) roasted almonds
  (or other nuts), crushed

Caramel
175 g (6 oz) caster (superfine) sugar
1 tablespoon lemon juice

❋ ⚘

Preheat the oven to 180°C (350°F).

Pour the milk into a saucepan and place over low heat. Add the star anise, cinnamon stick, vanilla seeds and salt. Heat for a few minutes to infuse the milk with the spices, stirring constantly, until fragrant. Turn off the heat and set aside. Remove the cinnamon stick and star anise.

In a bowl, whisk the eggs vigorously by hand until combined and frothy. Add the sugar, then whisk for another 2–3 minutes to dissolve the sugar and create a foamy mixture.

Gently pour the spiced milk over the eggs, mixing well with a whisk. Set aside.

To make the caramel, place the sugar, lemon juice and 2 tablespoons of water in a saucepan. Without stirring, warm the mixture over medium heat. When the caramel turns amber, turn off the heat and slowly stir in 1 tablespoon of cold water in a thin stream, taking great care not to burn yourself, as the hot caramel will splatter!

Pour a little caramel into six individual ramekins and refrigerate for a few minutes to harden. Pour the beaten egg mixture over the top.

Place the ramekins in a deep baking dish. Pour water into the dish until it comes halfway up the sides of the ramekins to create a water bath.

Transfer the baking dish to the oven and bake for 40 minutes, or until the creme caramel centres jiggle slightly, and a knife inserted in the middle of one comes out clean. Every 10 minutes or so, pour another 250 ml (1 cup) of cold water into the baking dish to cool the water bath.

Remove the baking dish from the oven, and remove the ramekins from the water bath. Leave to cool slightly, then refrigerate the creme caramels for 2–3 hours, until firm.

Serve in the ramekins, or inverted onto individual plates, sprinkled with the crushed almonds.

The creme caramels will keep in an airtight container in the fridge for 3–4 days.

DRINKS

I ALWAYS FEEL A PARTICULAR EMOTION
WHEN I TALK ABOUT BALKAN DRINKS.
LIKE MANY PEOPLE FROM THIS CORNER
OF THE WORLD, MY EARLIEST CHILDHOOD
MEMORIES ALMOST ALL REVOLVE
AROUND COFFEE.

It's not so much the drink itself that is so meaningful,
but rather the moments during which it is enjoyed.
The Balkan table wouldn't be complete without our
drinks. Alcoholic or not, they skilfully open and close
a good meal. In my family, they were all traditionally
prepared, from the plum-based aperitif to the lemonade
made with pomegranate or elderflower, and even wine.
Here I offer you a few recipes to try, some of which
are new creations, notably the cocktails created by
renowned mixologist Stephen Martin.

IBRIK COFFEE (CEZVE)

SERVES 1

15 g (½ oz) organic ground coffee
(or specialty coffee grounds for ibrik/
cezve)
granulated sugar, to taste

❋ 🌿

I will always remember
the smell that enveloped
us when my grandmother
made coffee in her ibrik.
It is partly thanks to
her that I embarked
on my great IBRIK
adventure with my cafe
and kitchen, originally
conceived as a 'coffee
shop'. While now a trendy
concept, this dream
has existed in my heart
since early childhood.

Heat 120 ml (4 fl oz) of water in a saucepan over medium heat until it reaches a temperature of 80°C (175°F), or until small bubbles are forming on the edge but the water isn't boiling.

Place the coffee in an ibrik and pour in half the hot water. Stir thoroughly to evenly disperse the coffee grounds and eliminate any bubbles. Pour in the remaining hot water and, if desired, sugar to taste (1 level teaspoon for lightly sweetened coffee, 2 teaspoons for sweet coffee and 1 tablespoon for very sweet).

Simmer the coffee over very low heat for 2–3 minutes, until a fairly firm crust forms on top. Remove from the heat before bubbles appear. (Coffee should never boil – if it boils and the crust disappears, it's burnt, and you'll have to start again.)

Pour into a coffee cup or glass and enjoy.

Note: *If you'd like, you can add spices along with the ground coffee – cardamom is especially good.*

SOCATĂ

SERVES 4-6

30 g (1 oz) fresh elderflowers
1 large lemon
100 g (3½ oz) granulated sugar
25 ml (¾ fl oz) lemon juice

Equipment

1 × 1.5 litre (6 cup) jar

Sterilise the jar by placing it in a large saucepan and adding water, until the jar is covered. Bring the water to the boil, then boil for 10 minutes. Let cool.

Wash the elderflowers and gently spin them dry. Remove the green stems, then place the elderflowers in the jar.

Using a sponge, rub the lemon under hot water, cleaning well. Dry thoroughly. Cut the lemon into very thin slices and add them to the jar.

In a bowl, mix together the sugar, lemon juice and 1 litre (4 cups) of fresh water. Pour the mixture into the jar, stirring gently.

Cover with a clean cloth or a small plate, then place the jar next to a heat source, or even in direct sunlight. Don't cover the jar tightly – you want the fermentation gases from the mixture to be able to escape.

Leave for 3 days, or until the socată is slightly sparkling.

Strain the contents through a sieve, then pour the socată into bottles. Seal and store in the fridge.

Serve in large glasses filled with ice, garnished with a few elderflowers, if desired.

The socată will keep in the fridge for up to 7 days.

POMEGRANATE
AND HIBISCUS INFUSION

SERVES 6

100 g (3½ oz) dried hibiscus flowers
2 pomegranates
½ bunch of mint, leaves picked
   (see Notes)

Fill a large saucepan with 1.5 litres (6 cups) of water. Add the hibiscus flowers and bring to the boil. Reduce the heat and simmer for 2 minutes. Turn off the heat and leave to steep for 20 minutes.

Strain the liquid into a large bowl and leave to cool. Discard the solids from the strainer.

Place the strainer back over the bowl. Cut the pomegranates in half and squeeze the juice into the bowl. Using a spoon, scoop the pomegranate seeds into the strainer and, using a ladle, press the seeds to release as much juice as possible into the bowl.

Pour the pomegranate juice and the cooled hibiscus infusion into a pitcher. Stir the mint leaves through, reserving a few for serving, and store in the fridge to chill.

Serve in tall glasses filled with ice, garnished with the reserved mint leaves.

The infusion will keep in an airtight container in the fridge for up to 3 days.

Notes: *Instead of mint, you can use grated fresh ginger, which you can steep with the hibiscus flowers.*

You can also turn this infusion into a marinade for red meat. Simply add olive oil, ginger and your favourite spices.

IBRIK

MORELLO CHERRY SERBET

SERVES ABOUT 20

500 g (1 lb 2 oz) fresh or frozen
  morello cherries, stemmed and pitted
1 kg (2 lb 3 oz) granulated sugar
pinch of salt
juice of ½ lemon

Equipment

2 × 450 ml (15 fl oz) jars with lids

Place a fine-mesh sieve over a bowl. Using a spoon or ladle, crush the cherries in the sieve to collect the juices.

Pour the cherry juice into a saucepan. Add the sugar, salt and 400 ml (13½ fl oz) of water and simmer over low heat until the sugar has completely dissolved, and the mixture resembles a syrup.

Bring to the boil and skim off any impurities that form on the surface. Reduce to a simmer to cook the syrup for 40–45 minutes until thickened but still pourable.

Turn off the heat, cover the saucepan with a damp clean tea towel, and leave to stand for 15 minutes, to let the syrup thicken.

Meanwhile, sterilise both jars by placing them in a saucepan and adding water, until the jars are covered. Bring the water to the boil, then boil for 10 minutes. Let cool.

Remove the towel from the saucepan with the syrup and stir the syrup in one direction with a wooden spoon until it turns pink and thickens. When the consistency is creamy, add the lemon juice and mix again until fully incorporated.

Pour the mixture into the jars, close the lids and leave to cool – it will solidify.

To serve, fill a glass with cold water and dip a spoonful of the solid serbet into it. It will not dissolve; serbet is eaten like a lollipop, enjoyed alongside the water.

The serbet will keep in the fridge for up to 1 month.

ICED CAPPUCCINO

SERVES 1

8 ice cubes
45 ml (1½ fl oz) cold double-shot
  espresso
sugar, for sweetening (optional)
200 ml (7 fl oz) cold skimmed milk
ground cinnamon, for sprinkling
  (optional)

✻ ⚘

Place half the ice cubes in a tall glass, then pour in the espresso. Add sugar to taste, stirring until it has dissolved.

Place the remaining ice cubes in a blender or shaker. Pour in the milk and blend or shake until frothy.

Pour the milk over the coffee and finish with a sprinkling of cinnamon, if desired.

VERMOUTH COCKTAIL

SERVES 1

50 ml (1¾ fl oz) gin
3 saffron threads
50 ml (1¾ fl oz) amber vermouth
  (Greek, preferably)
2 drops of kummel
3 drops of orange bitters
1 strip of mandarin peel

✻ ⚘

In a mixing glass, combine the gin and saffron, then leave to steep for 10 minutes. When a slight yellow–orange tinge appears, stir for a few seconds to further extract the saffron aromas.

Fill another mixing glass with ice. Add the vermouth, kummel, orange bitters and the saffron-infused gin. Using a cocktail spoon, stir everything together for 1 minute to allow all the liquids to blend.

Place two ice cubes in a wine glass. Place a cocktail strainer against the mixing glass and hold it firmly while pouring the vermouth mixture into the wine glass.

Gently twist the mandarin peel, drop it in the glass and serve.

ALOE VERA COCKTAIL

SERVES 1

40 ml (1¼ fl oz) vodka
30 ml (1 fl oz) aloe vera juice
30 ml (1 fl oz) coconut milk
30 ml (1 fl oz) almond milk
4–5 sprigs of coriander (cilantro)
coconut shavings, to garnish
dried rose petals, to garnish

✻ ⚘

Fill a cocktail shaker with ice cubes. Add the vodka, aloe vera juice, coconut milk and almond milk.

Strip the coriander leaves, then add to the shaker.

Shake vigorously for 1 minute to thoroughly emulsify the mixture, then strain into a stemmed cocktail glass.

Serve garnished with coconut shavings and rose petals.

IBRIK

ȚUICĂ SOUR

SERVES 1

20 ml (¾ fl oz) orange juice
20 ml (¾ fl oz) lemon juice
20 ml (¾ fl oz) cane sugar syrup
1 egg white
3 mint leaves, finely chopped
50 ml (1¾ fl oz) țuică (or palincă)
  (see Note)
ground turmeric, to garnish

Fill a shaker with ice cubes. Add the orange juice, lemon juice, cane sugar syrup, egg white and mint.

Shake vigorously for 1 minute to froth the egg whites.

Add the tuică, then shake again for another 1 minute.

Strain into a stemmed cocktail glass, garnish with turmeric and serve.

Note: *Țuică and palincă are plum brandies found mainly in Bulgaria, Romania and some former Yugoslavian countries. If you have trouble finding them, you can use any kind of plum brandy.*

TABLE OF RECIPES

INDEX

IBRIK

INDEX

Thanks to Raphaël de Montremy and
Thierry Nardy for lending me their
kitchen, and Saucisse and Fred for being
my first testers! I thank my children,
Estée and Léon, for their childlike
sincerity, sometimes cruel but life-saving.
Thank you also to my biggest fan,
Florian, for pushing me every day and
putting up with my madness. Thank you,
Mom, for giving me a taste for fresh
produce cooked with heart and patience,
and Dad, for allowing me to develop my
taste for the fine arts. And finally, thank
you, my team. Ibrik is your home.

First published in French in 2020 by Hachette Livre (Marabout)
Hachette Book 58, rue Jean-Bleuzen 92178 Vanves Cedex

This edition published in 2026 by Smith Street Books
Naarm | Melbourne | Australia
smithstreetbooks.com

Distributed outside of ANZ, North & Latin America by
Thames & Hudson Ltd., 6–24 Britannia Street, London, WC1X 9JD
thamesandhudson.com

EU Authorised Representative: Interart S.A.R.L.
19 rue Charles Auray, 93500 Pantin, Paris, France
productsafety@thameshudson.co.uk; www.interart.fr

ISBN: 978-1-923239-77-7

Smith Street Books respectfully acknowledges the Wurundjeri People of the Kulin Nation, who are the Traditional Owners of the land on which we work, and we pay our respects to their Elders past and present.

The moral right of the author has been asserted.

Publisher: Megan Cuthbert
Project editor: Avery Hayes
Editor: Katri Hilden
Cover and preliminary page designer: Emily O'Neill
Internal designer: Lila Theodoros
Layout: Heather Menzies, Studio31 Graphics
Photographer: Émilie Franzo
Proofreader: Ana Jacobsen
Indexer: Max McMaster
Prepress: Megan Ellis
Production manager: Aisling Coughlan

Printed & bound in China by C&C Offset Printing Co., Ltd.

Book 435
10 9 8 7 6 5 4 3 2 1

FSC
MIX
Paper | Supporting responsible forestry
www.fsc.org   FSC® C008047

Smith
Street
Books